Footprint

Costa de la Luz

Andy Symington

D1391000

Contents

Listings

Maps

About the author

Andy Symington is from Sydney, Australia. After studying some archaeology and psychology he became embroiled in the world of theatre administration and stage management. Moving into freelance journalism he lived in Edinburgh for two years selling whisky and wine and roaming the highlands before moving to northern Spain. He had his first glimpse of magical Cádiz as a six year old; since that early memory he has returned to the Costa de la Luz many times over the years, honing a healthy appetite for *manzanilla*, utterly failing to acquire the fundamentals of Andalucían horsemanship, and making valiant, but ultimately fruitless tilts at longstanding local tapas-eating records. Travel is a passion and he has spent much time in South America and north Africa as well as Europe; he also enjoys prowling around his native land. He is author of Footprint Bilbao, Seville, Andalucía and Northern Spain and is co-author of Footprint Spain.

Acknowledgements

As ever, in this project I have relied on the support of the team at Footprint, particularly editor Felicity Laughton, and Alan Murphy, who used his holidays to give valuable input on the region. I am also indebted to many friends, tourist office staff, bartenders and more, who have been generous with their local information. In particular, David Jackson and Reinhard Sahre are two friends who have accompanied me in the area on tapas-crawls that tested mind and body, while Montse Cuevas was a fantastic help with local knowledge. I also deeply thank my parents for constant support and encouragement, and Begoña for sharing the *manzanilla* and much more.

Introducing Costa de la Luz

The Costa de la Luz – the Coast of Light – has a wild, epic quality that never fails to thrill and astound the visitor. It's a world away from the other 'Costas', with very little development, and clean, sandy beaches that run for miles and miles and give astounding views as the setting sun pitches into the Atlantic. There's a feeling of freedom here, whether you're exploring the streets of vivid Cádiz or gazing at the African coast across the water; there's a feeling of space, as you roam the protected Coto Doñana wetlands or soar kitesurfing above the white-capped waves. Pleasures of the soul are indeed in abundance, but the flesh is well catered for too. Some of Spain's best seafood and most lovable tapas are to be found along this coast, while the crisp *manzanillas* and seductive *olorosos* will win you over even if you thought you didn't like sherry. It's a place that the chain hotels have largely bypassed; a place where you can run along the beach without hurdling towels and cans of lager; a windy and wonderful corner of Europe to feel vital again and appreciate the unspoiled charms of southern Spain.

Beyond the known world

For the ancients, the pillars of Hercules on either side of the Straits of Gibraltar marked the symbolic limits of the known world. This is where the calm Mediterranean, nursemaid and provider of civilizations, gave way to the Atlantic, unpredictable and temperamental as Poseidon himself. The Phoenicians braved it, founding cities and performing incredible navigational feats; we do not know how many boats they lost. This coast still has an untamed quality that you only get when an ocean is pounding away on your doorstep, pulverizing the coast into the whitest and cleanest of sand beaches, and testing human structures with a constant exhalation from interminably deep lungs. It was into this powerful deity that Columbus set sail in his three impossibly small ships; it was from here that laden ships emerged to elevate Cádiz to mercantile greatness; it is from this ocean that the tuna fishermen still harvest their giant catch. This is part of the magic of this coastline; to be on the edge of such inscrutable majesty.

Vitality

As well as light, it is a coast of motion. Even when you're lying still on the beach, the wind and the waves are never still; cue the elaborate twisting arcs you can perform when you kiss gravity goodbye for an instant kitesurfing and threaten briefly to join the birds in flight as they soar in migratory formation above. Cue the ripple of the running horse as you crest the dunes together and see Africa across the Straits or the whir of a tapas waiter pleasing the pre-lunch crowds in Cádiz or El Puerto de Santa María. Reprise the fluid grace of the choreographed *cartujano* horses; utter contrast to the boisterous bumping chaos of the Cádiz Carnaval, the passioned bobbing of the *simpecados* on the Rocío *romería*, or the modern white windfarms looking like alien arrivals with their whirling arms. The tortured, impassioned jerks and stamps of the flamenco dancer; the silken sweep of honey-coloured sherry into a glass: on this spirited coastline there is enough kinetic energy to recharge the most moribund of batteries.

At a glance

Cádiz

One of Europe's oldest cities, Cádiz was founded by the Phoenicians in the early first millennium BC. The city has an incredible situation on a long, narrow promontory. At the bulbous fingertip is the old town, an enchanting spiderweb of narrow maritime alleyways dotted with atmospheric *tabernas* and criss-crossed by bustling shopping streets. The *gaditanos* have a name for being some of Spain's most liberal folk. Its famous Carnaval isn't just exuberance and pageantry, although there's plenty of that, it also includes roaming minstrel groups whose biting satires on politicians and current events are eagerly awaited by the locals.

El Puerto de Santa María

Across the bay from Cádiz, this town, often known simply as El Puerto, has achieved cult status as a summer resort and lunch spot. Life focuses on its waterfront, a seafood boulevard, especially at weekends, when folk from Cádiz and Sevilla stroll around eyeing up likely crustaceans and molluscs. The historical if a little ramshackle centre also holds one of Spain's most prestigious bullrings. The city is one of the vertices of the 'sherry triangle', and several of the most famous *bodegas* can be found here.

Sanlúcar de Barrameda

It's difficult to exactly pin down why Sanlúcar is such an enchanting spot, but its undeniable appeal certainly has something to do with the pleasures of the palate. Mention Sanlúcar to any Spanish gastronome, and their eyes will cloud over with recalled pleasures in the terraced restaurants of the beachside barrio of Bajo de Guía. Crunchy seafood and crispy *manzanilla*, the local sherry, are a match made in heaven, but that's not all. The old town is a steep and narrow jumble of white streets, bustling plazas, and flamboyant palaces, while you can also

take boat tours from here to the Coto Doñana. In summer, it's
Ascot-on-the-Strand, as horses bolt down the beach.

Coto Doñana
This is one of Europe's most important protected areas and a vital
refuge for hundreds of species of bird, animal and plant. It divides
the Costa de la Luz in two; to travel from one side to the other, a
long detour via Sevilla is required. The park can only be entered on
a guided tour. On the edges, the village of El Rocío is home to one
of Spain's most revered virgins; its sandy streets – very Wild-West
like with wooden verandas and hitching rails for horses – fill at
Whitsun, when it's the culmination of a lively pilgrimage. Nearby,
the beach between Matalascañas and Mazagón is long, sandy,
clean and backed by protected dunes.

Lugares Colombinos
Beyond the national park are the intriguing 'Columbus towns',
where Cristóbal Colón (Christopher Columbus) dreamed up, kitted
out and embarked upon his first voyage of discovery across the
Atlantic. The voyage was a long time in the making, and the
monastery of La Rábida was where he petitioned for royal support,
helped by the savvy monks. It makes an interesting visit, and there
are replicas of the tiny ships he sailed in on the water below. He
actually set off from nearby Palos de la Frontera, where he also found
his sturdiest crewmembers; some also came from Moguer, a sleepy
town of noble buildings memorably wandered by Nobel-prize
winning writer Juan Ramón Jiménez and his donkey in Platero and I.

Jerez de la Frontera
Just half an hour from Cádiz, the largest city of the Costa de la Luz
couldn't be more different. The centre of the sherry industry is a
refined, genteel, traditional place whose historical links with Britain
make it Spain's capital of tweed and retrievers. Although it lacks
mind-blowing sights, it's a great place to visit, with some excellent

tapas and the world-famous Carthusian horses and their intricate dance steps. Contrastingly, Jerez is also home to a substantial gypsy population, and has a fabulous archive of recorded flamenco, as well as numerous bars in which to see it live.

White towns of Cádiz
More than anywhere, these hilltop settlements preserve traces of Moorish Spain. The Muslims brought North African urban planning with them across the Straits of Gibraltar; this meant coping with the intense heat by building compact whitewashed villages with narrow streets. These dazzling settlements, which can be seen for miles, are incredibly atmospheric to explore, all narrow winding lanes and little plazas with a wealth of elegant palaces and fantastic views.

South from Cádiz
The long stretch between Cádiz and Tarifa encompasses several of Spain's best beaches and has something for everyone, whether it's a family-friendly resort, a remote surfside campsite or a no-frills fishing town. The sandy stretches are long, white and clean and are backed by low, rolling hills. Other places, such as Bolonia or Los Caños de Meca, are only busy at the height of summer; at other times you'll have long beaches almost to yourself. Just inland, the white town of Vejer de la Frontera is a great place to wander and a fine spot to eat or sleep too.

Tarifa and around
The old town of this extremity of the Iberian peninsula feels distinctly Moorish, and it's no wonder, as the coast of Morocco is clearly visible across the Straits. The same wind that howls through the narrow streets has made the long sandy beach a favourite for windsurfers; more recently kitesurfing has grabbed the imagination and the euros of the folk that head here year-round to test themselves against wind and water. Tarifa is a curious mix of trendy and traditional; it's also a popular crossing point (no cars) to Morocco; you can even sample a *tagine* in Tanger and be back for dinner.

Trip planner

Furnished as it is with two fascinating cities as well as a very fine
national park, the Costa de la Luz has something for all times of the
year. Far from spoiled by tourism, the beaches hereabouts have,
nonetheless, long been popular with holidaying Spaniards in summer.
This means great nightlife in July and August, but also has the
associated higher accommodation prices and less peace and quiet.
The same is true of Semana Santa. A visit in May, June or September
practically guarantees good weather and will be much less frenetic.

24 hours

With only a day in hand, you should see something of either Cádiz or
Jerez, depending on what you're after. The former city would be ideal
as it combines a long, sandy town beach, museums, monuments,
enjoyable strolling in the old town and some excellent tapas bars to
enjoy, before moving to the 'pier' for late nightlife. In Jerez, you could
take in a sherry bodega, a display of intricate horsemanship and a
hearty, meaty meal in a restaurant by the bullring.

A long weekend

Spend at least a day in Cádiz; if you spend two, make sure you take
El Vaporcito across the bay to El Puerto de Santa María, having a
slap-up seafood lunch at Romerijo, or the train to Jerez to see some
fancy horses trot their stuff.

   After Cádiz, choose which segment of the coast you want to
discover. If you head south, you might stop for a night in the
hilltop town of Vejer and visit the nearby beaches of Los Caños de
Meca, while tucking into sea anemones in Barbate, then tuna
carpaccio at the wild strand of Zahara de los Atunes. In Tarifa you'll
have time for a lesson in the wild sport of kiteboarding.

   Alternatively, head northwest from Cádiz to Sanlúcar de Barrameda,
where the sea-salt tang of *manzanilla* will beguile you. From here you
can see one side of the Coto Doñana; an inland detour via Sevilla will

get you to the other side, where you can stay at the film-like village of El Rocío and watch birds on the adjacent *marismas* (marshes). Nearby you can discover the town of Moguer, where a Nobel-prize winner wandered with his donkey, and the monastery of La Rábida, where Columbus sweated over his funding applications.

A week or more

With a week on the Costa de la Luz, you can really see quite a lot of places; that is, if you don't just stay put and enjoy the beach and the sunshine of course! You can explore much of Cádiz; make sure you get to the Museo de Cádiz and at least the city's top five tapas bars; a night dancing late on the pier might be in order too. You can give the 'sherry triangle' the time it needs; especially charming Sanlúcar, its offbeat Museo del Mar and its waterside seafood restaurants; you might want to take a boat trip across to the national park of Coto Doñana.

Despite the lure of the sand, make sure you leave time to head inland to Arcos de la Frontera, where you can have a happy day wandering through art galleries, shops and narrow streets; and Medina Sidonia, where a cheap hearty lunch at Mesón Machín gives great views over the plains below.

Back at the coast, Conil de la Frontera is a great little town which goes about its business unspoiled by the visitors that enjoy its peaceful beach; nearby El Palmar has one of the most romantic seaside bars you're likely to see. Stand on the Cape of Trafalgar ponder the 15,000 lives lost to the seas below and watch tuna fishermen return with the catch at hard-working Barbate. If you fancy a night out, Janis Joplin gives her name to a much-loved late-opening bar in nearby Vejer de la Frontera.

Before reaching trendy Tarifa, chill out at the Roman ruins of Baelo Claudia and the spread-out beachside settlement of Bolonia. Once in Tarifa, you'll still have time for a kiteboarding course – five hours or so of lessons and you'll be striking out on your own – and maybe even a bit of whale-watching or a sly trip across the Straits to Morocco for the day.

Contemporary Costa de la Luz

Probably the most lovable aspect of the Costa de la Luz is the legendary amiability of the people, although the accent of Cádiz province can occasionally cause problems – even to other Spaniards. In this era of budget flights, interest in previously little-explored corners of western Europe is awakening, at the expense of the packaged beach holidays that were previously synonymous with a trip to the south of Spain, and the Costa de la Luz with all that it has to offer is benefiting.

There is significant optimism in places such as Sanlúcar, until recently one of Spain's poorest towns. A sudden surge in the *manzanilla* industry has seen its sales outstrip the more traditional dry sherry, *fino*, for the first time on record, and the town is beginning to buzz again. Jerez has embarked on an innovative process of regeneration to banish forever its undeserved mothball image, while Cádiz, since the fall of the dictatorship, has gone from strength to strength as its relaxed liberal outlook has allowed it to prosper in the new Europe. Another example is Tarifa, always a Cinderella looking enviously eastwards to the prosperity of Torremolinos or Marbella, whose resort status it was never going to emulate. Its beautiful beach was windy, and had breakers that were never going to seduce the paddlers of the Costa del Sol. Forward to the 21st century and Tarifa is one of the world capitals of windsurfing, is helping pioneer the thrilling sport of kitesurfing, is prosperous, popular year-round and has been spared the concrete monstrosities that dog resorts on the Mediterranean.

In some ways, the Costa de la Luz is one of Andalucía's last chances. The region has been hugely over-reliant on package tourism; in a 2002 article, the journalist Arturo Pérez Reverte famously lambasted, tongue firmly in cheek, the "traitorous foreigners" who were increasingly choosing other destinations for their fortnight in the sun. "How dare they? After we've even sacrificed the environment for them!" was the tone of his broadside against the thoughtless overdevelopment of large sections of the Andalucían coast. With prices higher after the conversion to the euro, and other charter destinations growing in popularity, the regional government has belatedly realized it perhaps should have been encouraging a more enlightened, sustainable tourism, and is taking steps in that direction, increasing protection levels for the region's natural parks and devoting more money to preservation of Andalucía's rich cultural and architectural heritage. The relatively unspoiled beaches of the Costa de la Luz will be an important barometer of just how committed the government is to safeguarding its natural inheritance. Spaniards, of course, have known about the Costa de la Luz for quite a while; El Puerto de Santa María and Mazagón have been favoured summering spots for many years. Places such as Los Caños de Meca or Zahara de los Atunes are becoming increasingly trendy, but more in a 'Zara-Beachwear' way than a cigar-smoking stroll along the promenade. And there's no way the locals are going to sell off the family silver to make a fast euro out of this potentially transient phenomenon; in the towns south of Cádiz, fishing still largely rules the roost. If you're enjoying your seafood dinner in Sanlúcar, that's because at six that morning a weathered old father-son team set out from the nearby harbour of Bonanza, filled their boat with what they could, then headed back to port and auctioned off their catch in the *lonja*; a fascinating sight. With both the Mediterranean and the Atlantic on their doorstep, there's an incredible variety available.

But the fishermen know these waters, and spend a significant proportion of their time tinkering with their boats, making sure they are seaworthy for these often treacherous waters. If only it were so with the *pateras* (p85). The Costa de la Luz is on the news more than weekly in Spain; the narrow and often treacherous Straits of Gibraltar are potentially the easiest way for Moroccans, Mauritanians, and Senegalese seeking a better life to cross to the El Dorado of the EU.

The proximity of Morocco has been a constant factor in the history of this area, and continues to have a substantial effect. Significant numbers of Moroccans along this coast work in the container terminals of Algeciras, Cádiz and Huelva, important ports all three, but all looking nervously across at Tanger, where the contstruction of a vast new hyper-port threatens to shift a lot of shipping business across to Africa with improved facilities and financial concessions. This, combined with the recent closure of several of Cádiz's shipyards (violently opposed, needless to say, by the thousands of employees), is the other side of the free-market coin that Spain has happily pocketed.

On the arts front, flamenco continues dominate. The form's revival was in a large part due to Camarón de la Isla, from the Cádiz area, and popularity continues to grow. Recently, flamenco has been combined with other music and produced flamenco-rock and flamenco-fusion; recent success stories include the flamenco chillout of Chambao and the beautiful collaboration of El Cigala with the Cuban pianist Bebo Valdés. Jerez is still regarded as one of the spiritual homes of flamenco, and contains the most important archive of the art.

Flamenco aslde,this southern corner of Andalucía doesn't have a cutting-edge contemporary music scene. Most bars and *discotecas* play a repetitive selection of Spanish pop, much of it derived from the phenomenally successful TV show *Operación Triunfo*, a star-creation program that spawned *Fame Academy* in the UK. In beach *chiringuitos* and *discotecas* the music tends to range from pop to *bacalao*, a general term for dance music; some are more latino in orientation, with salsa and merengue beats. The bars of the Costa de la Luz are a place to put musical snobbery aside and do as the locals do. It is often remarked that, no matter what personal troubles they may have, Andalucíans put on their happy faces to go out. At weekends, the crowded bars and *discotecas* are an uplifting scene, with singing along perfectly acceptable and dancing almost compulsory.

★   **Ten of the best**

Best

1   Barrio del Pópulo   A decayed and ultra-characterful little quarter; Cádiz's most enchanting barrio, filled with old fishermen's houses, quirky shops and staunchly local bars, p39.

2   Museo de Cádiz   Probe the history and archaeology of one of Europe's most ancient cities, and upstairs, contemplate the dark beauty of some of the finest of Spain's Golden Age of painting, p41.

3   Bodegas   Visit a sherry winery in El Puerto de Santa María, Sanlúcar de Barrameda or Jerez. Revel in the glorious musty smell of aging wine and enjoy a generous tasting, p47, 52 and 76.

4   Bajo de Guía   Crisp *manzanilla* and crunchy crustaceans; a match made in heaven; the best place to enjoy them is in Sanlúcar's fishermen's barrio, with outdoor tables, sun and sand, p52.

5   El Rocío   So Wild West it deserves a Morricone score, the sandy streets of El Rocío attract wildlife lovers year-round to the adjacent Coto Doñana, and Spain's most revelrous Whitsun pilgrimage, p58.

6   Centro Andaluz de Flamenco   A must for any lover of flamenco; this archive in Jerez has a wealth of catalogued recordings and footage of all the great artists, p74.

7   Arcos de la Frontera   A white town shining out from above high and seriously perpendicular cliffs. Its tortuous streets and noble buildings are a delight to explore, p78.

8   El Palmar   This surf beach south of Conil de la Frontera is for lovers of sand simple. There's one place to stay, two places to eat and drink, and it's all memorable, p82.

9   Vejer de la Frontera   Few towns preserve as much of the character of Moorish Spain as this one, and there are few better-value places to sleep and eat than its labyrinthine Casa del Califa, p86.

10   Kitesurfing   Learn this exhilarating sport at Tarifa. Defy gravity as you soar bird-like above the waves, all with the African coast in clear view, p184.

The best way of reaching the Costa de la Luz is by air. Although the international airport at Jerez de la Frontera deals with few flights, the busier airports of Málaga and Sevilla are within easy reach by hire car or public transport.

Flight prices are much higher in summer and at Christmas and Easter than at other times of the year. Booking well in advance is advisable at these times or you'll get stuck with a ludicrous full-fare ticket.

While the major destinations on the coast such as Cádiz, Jerez, and Tarifa are all well connected by regular bus, if you want to explore some of the more isolated beachside locations, by far your best bet is to hire a car on arrival. While local transport does connect everywhere, if your stay is a short one it seems foolish to waste time waiting for the only bus of the day, or planning your whole trip around timetables. Cars can be hired at very competitive rates at all three airports.

Getting there

Air

From Europe The closest airport to the Costa de la Luz is Jerez de la Frontera (XRY), reached by a **Ryanair** flight from London Stansted two to three times daily. Ryanair also serves Sevilla, which is handy for the northern part of the Costa de la Luz, while there are numerous budget connections from the UK to Málaga, two to three hours away by public transport.

Among operators from the UK, **Easyjet** fly to Málaga from seven British airports (Bristol, East Midlands, Liverpool, Newcastle, London Gatwick, Stansted and Luton). **Flybe** operate from Exeter and Southampton, while **BmiBaby** operate out of Cardiff, East Midlands, Manchester and Teeside. **Air Scotland** fly from Edinburgh and Glasgow, as do **FlyGlobespan**. From Ireland, **AerLingus** connect Dublin and Sevilla, while AerLingus, **Ryanair**, and **EUJet** link Málaga with Dublin, Cork, and Shannon.

Fares for all these flights can fall as low as £40-50 return off season or with advance booking, but can rise to £130 or much more in summer. In this constantly changing world of low-cost operators, a useful website is **www.whichbudget.com**, which keeps track of who flies where.

There are numerous charter flights to Málaga (and some to Almería) from many British and Irish airports. These flights can fall as low as £80 return out of season, but are normally £120-150 in spring and summer. **Avro** is one of the best charter flight companies, but be sure to check the travel pages of newspapers for cheap deals. **Monarch Airlines** often have cheap fares through travel agencies.

Málaga again has the most scheduled flights, with several airlines including **Iberia** and **British Airways** flying direct from London airports. There are daily direct flights to Sevilla codeshared by Iberia and British Airways from London Heathrow and Gatwick, as well as numerous opportunities for connections via Madrid and

→ Airlines and travel agents

Air Canada, www.aircanada.ca, T 1 888 2472262.
Aer Lingus, www.aerlingus.com, T 01-886 8888 (Ireland).
Air Europa, www.air-europa.co.uk, T 0870 240 1501 (UK).
Air France, www.airfrance.com/uk, www.airfrance.fr,
T 0845 0845 111(UK), T 1 800 237 2747 (USA).
Air Scotland, www.air-scotland.com.
American Airlines, www.aa.com, T 1 800 433 7300 (USA).
Basiq Air, www.basiqair.com.
BMI, www.flybmi.com, T 0845 60 70 555 (UK).
BmiBaby, www.bmibaby.com.
British Airways, www.ba.com, T 0845 77 333 77 (UK),
T 1 800 247 9297 (USA).
Delta, www.delta.com, T 1 800 221 1212 (USA).
Easyjet, www.easyjet.com, T 0870 6 000 000 (UK).
German Wings, www.germanwings.com.
Flybe, www.flybe.com.
Globespan, www.flyglobespan.com.
Hapag-Lloyd Express, www.hlx.com,
Iberia, www.iberia.com, T 020 8222 8970 (UK), T 01 407 3018
(Ireland), T 1 800 772 4642 (USA).
KLM, www.klmuk.com, T 0345 777 666 (UK).
Lufthansa, www.lufthansa.co.uk, T 0845 7737 747 (UK).
Ryanair, www.ryanair.com, T 0871 246 0000 (UK),
T 01 609 7800 (Ireland).
Snowflake, www.flysnowflake.com.
Spanair, www.spanair.es, T 902 131 415 (Sp).
Sterling, www.sterlingticket.com.

Barcelona. The cost for these flights is about £100-230 depending
on season and pre-booking. Flight time is around two hours 40
minutes non-stop from London.

US Airways, www.usairways.com, **T** 1 800 428 4322 (USA).
Virgin Express www.virgin-express.com.

Budget travel agents
Flight Centre, www.flightcentre.com.au, **T** 133 133, 580;
www.flightcentre.co.nz, **T** 0800 243 544. Budget flight shop with
many branches throughout Australia and New Zealand.
STA Travel, Specialists in student and budget travel. Branches all
over the UK, www.statravel.co.uk, **T** 0870 1 600 599; USA and
Canada, www.statravel.com, **T** 1 800 781 4040; Australia,
www.statravel.com.au, **T** 1 300 733 035; and New Zealand
www.statravel.co.nz.
Trailfinders, www.trailfinders.co.uk, www.trailfinders.ie,
www.trailfinders.com.au. Reliable budget travel specialists.
Travel Cuts, www.travelcuts.com, **T** 1 866 246 9762. A good
Canadian budget travel agent with offices all across the country.

Online operators
www.avro.com.
www.cheapflights.co.uk.
www.easyvalue.com.
www.ebookers.com.
www.expedia.co.uk, www.expedia.com.
www.lastminute.com.
www.opodo.com.
www.travelocity.com.

British Airways also fly daily from London and Manchester to
Gibraltar, 50 km east of Tarifa. The airport is at the entrance to the
colony. (Intriguingly you have to cross the runway to enter the

town; there's no cross-border transport between Spain and Gibraltar so, unless you hire a car at Gibraltar airport, you have walk over the border to the Spanish town of La Línea. From La Línea, there are regular buses to Algeciras and on to Tarifa.)

Two useful flight comparison tools are **www.easyvalue.com** and **www.kelkoo.co.uk**.

Air Berlin and their partner **Hapag-Lloyd** operate flights several times weekly to Jerez from a large number of German, Austrian, and Swiss cities. These prices can be as low as €200, but in summer can be much more expensive than their non-budget counterparts. A similar range of Air Berlin flights go to Sevilla, while there are numerous scheduled budget and charter flights to Málaga with such airlines as **Sterling** (from Denmark, Sweden, and Norway), **Virgin Express** (from many European countries via their Brussels hub), **Snowflake** (Denmark), and **Jet Only** (Belgium).

There are daily non-stop flights to Seville from Paris Orly (3 a day, operated by **Air France/Iberia**) and from Brussels (**SN Brussels Airlines**). These fares tend to hover around €250-300 but can be substantially lower with offers or out of season. Flying from these or other western European cities via Madrid or Barcelona is usually about the same. Cheaper flights are available to Málaga, destination of numerous charter flights and focus of special offers from the mainstream airlines throughout the year.

From North America There are no direct flights from North America to any Andalucían airport, so you'll have to connect via Madrid, Barcelona, London or another European city. From the east coast, flights can rise well over US$1,000 in summer but, in winter or with advance purchase, you can get away with as little as US$500. Prices from the west coast are usually only US$100 or so more. **Iberia** flies direct to Madrid from many east coast cities and **British Airways** often offers reasonable add-on fares via London. Although some airlines throw in a free connecting flight to Málaga or Sevilla, you can usually save considerably by flying to Madrid and getting the bus down south. Travellers from Canada will usually find that it's cheaper to fly to Andalucía via London than Madrid.

Airport information **Jerez's airport** (XRY), much the handiest for the Costa de la Luz, is 8 km northeast of town off the Sevilla road. **T** 956 150 083 for airport information. There's currently no bus service to the airport; a taxi to or from the centre should cost around €10-13. Car rental is available through Hertz and Atesa.

Sevilla's airport (SVQ) is located 10 km northeast of the city centre. There are the usual facilities, including a tourist information kiosk and several car hire companies. A bus runs to and from the airport to central Sevilla (€1.20) via the train stations, where you can connect to Jerez and Cádiz. It goes roughly every half hour on weekdays and is designed to coincide with International flights. There are plenty of taxis; a fare to the city is currently €21 during the day, slightly more at night or on public holidays.

Málaga Airport (AGP), **T** 952 048 844, handles nearly eight million passengers a year and is located some 7 km west of the city centre. The international terminal has two levels, with arrivals on the ground floor and departures on the first floor. All the main international firms are represented here, plus a few local firms. There is a tourist information office in the arrivals hall. The quickest way to the Costa de la Luz is to get the small train from the airport into Málaga station, then walk the short distance to the bus station, from where there are connections to Cádiz, Jerez, and Tarifa. There is also an airport bus (€1) to and from the bus station.

Car

The Costa de la Luz is over 2,000 km from London by road; a dedicated drive will get you there in 20-24 driving hours. By far the fastest route is to head down the west coast of France, to Madrid via Bilbao then south via Córdoba and Sevilla. Cars must be Insured for third party, and practically any driving licence is acceptable. Tolls on motorways in France and Northern Spain will add

→ Travel extras

Safety Andalucía is a very safe place to travel. There's been a crackdown in recent years and what tourist crime there is tends to be of the opportunistic kind: robberies from parked cars or the occasional snatch-and-run theft from vehicles stopped at traffic lights. If parking in a city or a popular hiking zone, try to make it clear there's nothing to nick inside a car by leaving the glovebox open, etc. If you are unfortunate enough to be robbed, you should report the theft immediately at the nearest police station, as insurance companies will require a police statement.

Police There are three types of police: Guardia Civil, a national force dressed in green, are responsible for the roads, borders and law enforcement away from towns; Policía Nacional, brown-shirted folk, are responsible for most urban crimefighting; these are the ones to go to if you need to report anything stolen, etc; and Policía Local/ Municipal, present in large towns and cities, are responsible for some urban crime, as well as traffic control and parking.

Tipping Far from compulsory, but much practised in Spain, a 10% tip is considered fairly generous in a restaurant, but not excessive. Closer to the Spanish norm would be 5%. It's rare for a service charge to be added to a bill. Waiters do not normally expect tips for lunchtime set meals or tapas, but here and in bars and cafés people will often leave small change, especially for table service. Taxi drivers don't expect a tip, but don't expect you to sit around waiting for 20 cents change either. In rural areas, churches will often have a local keyholder who will open it up for you; if there's no admission charge, a tip or donation is appropriate, say €0.50-1 per head, more if they've given a detailed tour.

significantly to your costs; petrol costs €0.85-0.95 per litre in Spain. Driving conditions in Spain are very good.

Coach
The quickest way to get to the Costa de la Luz from Britain by bus is with **Eurolines** (www.eurolines.co.uk) to Madrid, then an interurban bus to Cádiz (€18 each way, 7½ hours). The London-Madrid sector takes 26-28 hours and costs around £120 return, although this can fall to £72 if booked a month in advance out of season. Eurolines also run a Paris-Sevilla service.

Train
Unless you've got a railpass or you aren't too keen on planes, forget about getting to Sevilla by train from anywhere further than France; you'll save no money over the plane fare and use up days of time better spent learning to kitesurf. You'll have to connect via Sevilla and either Barcelona (three trains daily, 10-12 hours, €48.50-66.50) or Madrid (10-21 AVE fast trains daily, two hours 25 minutes, €64). Getting to Madrid/Barcelona from London takes about a day using **Eurostar** (www.eurostar.com, **T** 0870 160 6600); count on £100-200 return to Paris, and another €130 or more return to reach Madrid/Barcelona from there. Using the ferry across the channel adds eight or more hours and saves up to £100.

Getting around

Bus
The best form of public transport for getting around the Costa de la Luz region is bus. The principal hub for most of the area is Cádiz, The main bus station in Cádiz is just off Plaza de España, **T** 956 807 059. The main company is **Comes,** who run hourly buses to Sevilla (one hour 45 minutes, €9.10). Málaga is targeted six times a day (four hours); Madrid is served six times daily

(€21.50, eight hours) by a different company, **Secorbus**, who run from Plaza Helios near the football stadium not far from the Carranza bridge in the new town.

Within the Costa de la Luz region, Comes runs half-hourly buses to Jerez (40 minutes, €2.50), five a day to Tarifa (one hour 30 minutes), and six to 10 to Conil and Barbate, both drop-off point for places in-between such as Los Caños de Meca. There are four buses daily to Zahara de los Atunes. Inland, Vejer de la Frontera is hit five to nine times a day, Arcos de la Frontera is reached three to six times daily, and Medina Sidonia five times.

Los Amarillos, **T** 956 285 852, run from just near the tourist office on Av Ramón de Carranza to Chipiona via El Puerto de Santa María (40 minutes, €2.50) and Sanlúcar de Barrameda (one hour 15 minutes, €2.55) 11 times on weekdays and five times on weekends.They also run two to five buses to Arcos de la Frontera (one hour, €3.78).

For the Coto Doñana region, things are a bit trickier. You'll have to journey inland to Sevilla, change bus station from Prado de San Sebastián to Plaza de Armas, and then get a bus out to El Rocío and Matalascañas (three daily, one hour 30 minutes, €6.50-7); for Mazagón, it's easier to head to Huelva and change there for six daily buses, as only one bus runs along the coast from Matalascañas.

Of the towns, the only one that is challenging to negotiate on foot is Cádiz, which is forced by geography into being very long and thin. While the old town is reasonably compact, the new town is not. Bus No 1 runs every five minutes from the Plaza de España right down the length of the new town. A journey in a cab from the old town to the bars of the Paseo Marítimo should cost around €5; if you can't find one at one of the plentiful ranks, call **T** 956 212 121.

In Jerez, local bus No 10 runs from the train and bus stations into the centre; otherwise about a 15-minute walk.

Boat

El Vaporcito is a boat that runs from Cádiz across to Puerto de Santa María four times a day and back (six in summer). The trip takes 40 minutes and gives great views of the city. Tickets are €2.50 single/€4.50 return. The boat doesn't run on Monday from mid-September to mid-May. **T** 629 468 014 for information. For information on ferries from Tarifa to Morocco, see Tours, p28.

Car

Unless you're planning to base yourself wholly in cities such as Cádiz, Jerez and Tarifa, it makes a lot of sense to hire a car (see p200). None of the towns of the Costa de la Luz are especially hard to navigate or park in (except Sanlúcar de Barrameda!), and car-hire rates are low in this part of Spain because of the competition. The cheapest place to hire a car is Málaga airport, where rates can come down to €80 a week off-season with Internet deals; Star is one of the cheapest operators. More normal Spanish prices hover around €40/140 for a day/week. Shop around on the Internet though, as many 'budget car hire' sites simply reserve the car in your name with one of the big companies, and charge you a fee on top. Rates are also reasonable at Jerez and Sevilla airports. Check the websites for weekend or week-long deals. Petrol in Spain costs €0.85-0.95 per litre.

Cycling

The Costa de la Luz is a good area for cycling. Although distances are long and winds can be discouraging, there are particularly beautiful stretches between Conil and Zahara de los Atunes, and in the Coto Doñana between El Rocío and Mazagón. Both these avoid main roads and maximize the region's appeal. Cycling around busy Cádiz or baking Jerez is less appealing.

Cycling presents a curious contrast; Spaniards are mad for the competitive sport, but essentially uninterested in cycling as a means of transport. Thus there are plenty of cycling shops (although beware; it can be time-consuming to find replacement parts for non-standard cycles) but very few bike lanes. Taking your own bike to Andalucía is well worth the effort as most airlines are happy to accept them, providing they come within your baggage allowance. Bikes can be taken on trains, but have to travel in the guard's van and must be registered. Contact the **Real Federación de Ciclismo en España**, www.rfec.com, for more links and assistance.

Train

There is one useful train line in the region, and this links the cities of Sevilla and Cádiz via Jerez de la Frontera and El Puerto de Santa María. Trains run about a dozen times daily between Sevilla and Cádiz (1 hour 45 minutes, €8.40 on standard service) and there are half-hourly *cercanía* connections from Cádiz to El Puerto de Santa María (35 minutes) and Jerez (45-50 minutes). Some of the Sevilla-bound trains connect with trains to Málaga at the junction of Dos Hermanas.

Tours

Boat

Numerous travel agencies offer day trips from Tarifa to Morocco on the ferry; these include a guided visit to Tanger and lunch and cost around €49. There are more elaborate options involving overnight stays, and trips to Fez and Marrakech.

Bus

In **Cádiz** there are two companies running the standard open-top bus tours around the city. Both leave from Plaza San Juan de Dios and throw in a walking tour.

There's a hop-on hop-off double-decker bus tour of **Jerez**, whose main stop is outside the tourist office on Plaza del Arenal. It runs Wednesday to Sunday and costs €8. **T** 954 560 693 for information.

Coto Doñana

4WD bus tours of the park run daily from the visitors' centre at **El Acebuche** at 0830 and 1500 year round except Monday in winter. They last four hours and cost €19.50 per person. It is essential to reserve in advance, **T** 959 430 432, or at the centre itself. At short notice, you stand a much better chance midweek; during holiday periods, you should allow a few weeks to get a seat.

These tours sometimes pick up people who have booked from Sanlúcar; they get ferried across by a launch, **T** 959 448 711 to enquire; again, you need to do this well in advance.

Marismas de Doñana, **T** 629 060 545, run small tours to some of the more isolated parts of the park in the morning and evening and will collect you from your hotel. The trip costs €21.

The *Real Fernando* is a chunky old boat that runs trips from Sanlúcar de Barrameda across to the Coto Doñana. These depart daily at 1000; and also at 1600 (April, May, October) and 1700 (June-September). The trip takes 3½ hours and includes two stops. You can rent binoculars on board (€3). It's essential to reserve a place as far in advance as you can (**T** 956 363 813, www.visitas donana. com). The boats leave from opposite the building, and the trip costs €14.64 for adults and €7.32 for five to 12 year olds.

General

Girasol, Calle Colón 12, Tarifa, **T** 652 868 929, www.glrasol-adventure.com. Tarifa-based set-up running walking, horse riding, climbing, and mountain-biking excursions in the region.

Horse riding

For riding tours around the forests and beaches of the Costa de la Luz, see p183.

Whale- and dolphin-watching

Two major organizations that run whale- and dolphin-watching trips out of Tarifa are **FIRMM**, Calle Pedro Cortés 4, **T** 956 627 008, www.firmm.org; and **Whale Watch España**, Avenida de la Constitución 6, **T** 956 627 013. Trips should be booked the day before and they won't leave unless they have enough people. They charge about €22; you are more or less guaranteed to see dolphins and possibly pilot whales, depending on the season. FIRMM offer you another trip for free if you don't see anything.

Wine and food

Euroadventures, Calle Velásquez Moreno 9, Vigo, Spain **T**+34 986 221 399, www.euroadventures.net. A range of interesting tours, many focusing on food and wine, including the bodegas of Jerez.
Epiculinary Tours, **T**+1 847 295 5363, www.epiculinary.com. Tours to delight foodies, with lessons on making tapas and other Andalucían food interspersed with plenty of tastings and cultural visits.
Blackheath Wine Trails, 13 Blackheath Village, London SE3 9LA. Bodega tours based at Jerez de la Frontera.

Tourist information

The tourist information infrastructure is generally excellent, with a wide range of information, often in English, German and French as well as Spanish. All offices will be able to provide a map of the town and a list of registered accommodation. Staff are not allowed to make recommendations. If you're in a car, it's especially worth asking for a listing of rural accommodation (*casas rurales*).

Arcos de la Frontera

The tourist office is in the heart of town on Plaza del Cabildo, **T** 956 702 264, Monday to Saturday 1000-1500, 1600-2030 (winter all day 1000-1900), Sunday 1030-1500. There are guided tours of the town (€3) in Spanish leaving Monday to Friday 1030, 1200, 1700, 1830, Saturday 1030, 1200.

Barbate

The tourist office is at Calle Vásquez Mella 2, **T** 956 433 962, turismo@aytobarbate.org, Monday to Friday 0800-1430 all year. From May to September they open a kiosk on the Paseo Marítimo (s/n), daily 1000-1400, 1600-2000.

Cádiz

The helpful Junta de Andalucía tourist office is handily located at Calle Nueva s/n, **T** 956 258 646, Tuesday to Friday 0900-1900, Monday and Saturday 0900-1400. Nearby is the municipal office Plaza de San Juan de Dios 11, **T** 956 241 001, Monday to Friday 0900-1400, 1700-2000. At weekends it transfers itself to a small kiosk outside, Saturday and Sunday 1000-1330, 1600-1800 (1700-1900 summer).

El Puerto de Santa María

The tourist office near the boat dock, Calle Luna 22, **T** 956 542 413, daily 1000-1400, 1730-1930 October to April, 1800-2000 May to September, can furnish you with a town map and helpful printed sheets of accommodation, transport, tapas routes, etc.

Jerez de la Frontera

The city has two handy tourist offices, both open Monday to Friday 1000-1500, 1630-1830, Saturday and Sunday 0930-1430 (1530 in summer), one is on the central Plaza del Arenal, and the other is at the other end of the principal shopping street Calle Larga, where it joins the main avenue Alameda Cristina.

Mazagón

The tourist office, Monday to Friday 1000-1400, 1700-2000, in the police station in the heart of town, can provide limited information on the region.

Matalascañas

The tourist office, Avenida de las Adelfas s/n, T 959 430 286, Monday to Friday 0930-1400, Saturday 1000-1400 (longer hours in high summer), is at the entrance to the Parque Dunar on the west edge of town (if arriving by car from the north, head straight across the roundabout following signs for the beach).

Sanlúcar de Barrameda

The tourist office, Calzada de Ejército s/n, T 956 366 110, daily 1000-1400, 1600-1800 (1800-2000 summer), is located on the long avenue descending to the beach from near Plaza de Cabildo. It's a dream, with well-prepared information sheets on the town. There's also an information desk in the Fábrica de Hielo (p52); this is also the place to book trips into the Parque Nacional Coto Doñana.

Tarifa

The tourist office, Paseo de la Alameda s/n, T 956 680 993, turismo.tarifa@teleline.es, daily 0830-1500, summer 1000-2100, is just outside the old town. They have plenty of lists of accommodation, tour operators and watersports companies.

Vejer de la Frontera

The helpful tourist office is at Avenida los Remedios, T 956 450 191, Monday to Friday 0800-1500, 1700-2000 (Saturday and Sunday 1100-1400 in July and August only), in the heart of the old town, in a former marquis' palace. They'll give out a large paper map, but ask them for the glossy brochure as well, which has more information on the sights around the place.

Cádiz

Cádiz is situated on a long narrow promontory with the Atlantic on one side and the Bahía de Cádiz on the other. The old town occupies the tip of the promontory; the extensive new town stretches several kilometres along the main town beach, Playa de la Victoria.

With a proud and long maritime history stretching back to the Phoenicians, it comes as no surprise that Cádiz can seem less conservative and more outward looking than many Andalucían cities; geographically it's not far off being an island, and culturally it's typified by its riotous Carnaval (see box, p168). Earthquakes and buccaneering have deprived it of a significant collection of monuments, but it's a very likeable place with the sea seemingly at the end of every narrow street. The architecture of the old town is a quiet and elegant blend of 18th- and 19th-century houses, while beyond the old city gates stretches the interminable Avenida de Andalucía, which runs parallel to the town's long beaches and has plenty of nightlife options along it.

▸▸ *See Sleeping p97, Eating and drinking p121, Bars and clubs p147*

While the old town is reasonably compact, the new town is not. Bus No 1 runs every five minutes from the Plaza de España right down the length of the new town. A journey in a cab from Plaza San Juan de Dios in the old town to the bars of the Paseo Marítimo should cost €4-5. There are plenty of ranks; otherwise T 956 212 121.

◉ Sights

One of the charms of Cádiz is simply wandering around its maze of narrow streets; the houses typically have glassed-in balconies. Barrio del Pópulo, to the east of the cathedral, is one of the most traditional districts, as is Barrio de la Viña, the blocks behind Castillo de San Sebastián. One of the streets here, Calle Pastora, is picturesquely festooned with flowerpots.

La Catedral

Plaza de la Catedral s/n, and Plaza de Fray Felix s/n, **T** 956 259 812. *Tue-Fri 1000-1400, 1630-1930, Sat 1000-1300, Sun 1100-1300, €3, including entry to museum (cathedral only, free).* Torre de Poniente **T** 956 251 788, *daily 1000-1730 (1930 in summer), entry by guided tour every half hour, €3. Map 1, E8, p251*

Especially picturesque when viewed from further around the waterfront, with its golden dome glinting, Cádiz's cathedral was built in the 18th and 19th centuries. Its main façade on Plaza de la Catedral is a blend of the late Baroque and the neoclassical and flanked by two graceful white towers. The interior is rather sombre, reminding one more than anything of a Roman necropolis, with huge Corinthian columns looming in the shadows. A fine feature is the wonderful choir of cedar and mahogany, with carved figures of saints. The crypt below is a brilliantly realized space in sombre stone; the architectural precision is reflected by the astonishing echoes produced. Here is buried the *gaditano* composer Manuel de Falla (see box, p38).

Also worth looking out for are the elegant sacristy and a large monstrance used in the sober Corpus Christi processions. The effect of the high central dome is rather ruined by the netting which protects visitors from falling masonry.

Entry to the cathedral includes admission to its museum, tucked around the side on Plaza de Fray Felix. This is set in a charming building with an old columned patio that is of rather more interest than the artwork, particularly as part of an excavated Roman road runs through it. Of the paintings on display, a picture of the fierce Anglo-Dutch sack of the town in 1596 stands out, as do two 16th-century works of the *Judas Kiss* and the *Crowning of Thorns*. Some massive 16th- to 19th-century pergamines sit in a large bookcase; in the same room is a letter from Sta Teresa to the Inquisitor-General sealed in an ivory reliquary. A collection of carved 17th- to 18th-century ivory crucifixes show fine craftsmanship.

A scribble of white on a sheet of blue glass,
lying curved on the bay like a scimitar and
sparkling with African light

Laurie Lee, describing Cádiz in
As I Walked Out One Midsummer Morning

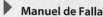

Manuel de Falla

In the crypt of Cádiz cathedral is the tomb of perhaps Spain's finest composer, Manuel de Falla, who was born in the city in 1870. After moving to Madrid, he came under the influence of Felipe Pedrell, largely responsible for the revival of Spanish music in the late 19th century. Here he taught piano, and his one-act opera *La Vida Breve*, set in Granada, won a presitigious composition prize. He then moved to Paris, where among his friends were Ravel and Debussy. He wrote several chamber works here, including *Noches en los jardines de España* (Nights in the Gardens of Spain).

De Falla returned to Spain when the First World War began, and lived here, mostly in Granada, until 1939. His ballet *El sombrero de tres picos* (The Three-Cornered Hat) was highly successful in London. Commissioned by Diaghilev, the set was designed by Picasso. Another success was his opera *El amor brujo* (Bewitching Love), set in Cádiz. In Granada he became a friend and mentor to Federico García Lorca, and the two collaborated to stage the famous 1922 *Cante jondo* competition in an effort to preserve the important Andalucían flamenco traditions. De Falla was profoundly interested in Andalucían culture and history, and many of his compositions were based on traditional folk songs.

Deeply religious, de Falla lived a curious life in Granada. He was an obsessive hypochondriac who used to spend four hours washing hImself every morning and who irrigated himself at least twice a day with his enema. His house on the Alhambra hill is one of Andalucía's most fascinating small museums.

Disgusted with the Civil War, in which his strong pro-Catholic feelings clashed with his hatred of fascism and left him unable to support either side, he left for Argentina, where he died in 1946.

One of the cathedral's towers, the **Torre de Poniente**, can be climbed. This takes the form of a guided tour with some information on the city. There are views out over the Atlantic and along the coast.

Barrio del Pópulo
Map 1, D9, p251

This was the heart of medieval Cádiz and is a small network of crumbling buildings and narrow streets. On the Plaza de la Catedral, look out for the gateway with embrasures that marks the entrance to the district. Near the cathedral on the waterfront is a **Roman theatre** (*Tue-Sun 1000-1400, free*), dating to the first century BC, while on Calle San Juan de Dios is another of the gateways to the barrio, as well as a stretch of the old walls. The later walls, built after the attack of 1596, have mostly been taken down.

At the edge of this barrio, the Plaza San Juan de Dios is dominated by the attractive **Ayuntamiento** (town hall), a typical example of neoclassical *gaditano* architecture. Not far from here, there is a beautiful former tobacco factory in Moorish style, dating from 1741. Further south is the principal entrance to the city, the 18th-century **Puerta de Tierra**. It marks the boundary of the old and new towns and is one of the only bits of the city wall still standing.

! Cádiz's old town looked similar enough to Havana for it to be chosen as the setting for some scenes of the James Bond movie *Die Another Day*.

Barrio de la Viña
Map 1, F5, p250

Moving the other way from the cathedral, and following the waterfront, with rocks pounded by the Atlantic, you'll pass another historic barrio on your right, the Barrio de la Viña, before reaching the **Castillo de San Sebastián**. This fort is set on a small islet (it was joined by a causeway to the mainland in the 19th century) where some say the Phoenician temple of Melqart-Hercules once stood. It's a relaxing walk out to the castle, now a lighthouse, but you can't enter the building itself.

Beyond is another castle, **Santa Catalina**, built after the British attack on the city. Constructed in a star-shape to maximize firing arcs, it also contains a small chapel. Between the two castles is the rather ordinary **Playa de la Caleta**, backed by two massive dragon trees.

Plaza de la Mina and around
Map 1, B5, p250

In the north part of the old town, Plaza de la Mina is a large square around which are many of the city's best tapas and drinking bars. On the square itself is the excellent Museo de Cádiz (see below). On the south side of the square a plaque marks the house where the composer Manuel de Falla (see p38) was born.

Just east of here is another pleasant square, **Plaza San Francisco**, while to the south the larger **Plaza San Antonio** is dominated by its twin-towered Baroque church. North of Plaza de la Mina are the very soothing waterside gardens, the **Alameda Marqués de Comillas**, which end at a defensive gun battery. East of the gardens, the large **Plaza de España** is marked by a monument to the Cortes Liberales de Cádiz.

Museo de Cádiz

Plaza de la Mina s/n, **T** 956 212 281. *Tue 1430-2000, Wed-Sat 0900-2000, Sun 0930-1430, free for EU citizens, €1.50 for others. Map 1, A5, p250*

This excellent museum, one of the best in Andalucía, comprises both an archaeological and a fine arts section. The former, on the ground floor, is particularly notable for its Phoenician collection, with many finds from tombs in Cádiz and the surrounding area. It is known that there was an important temple of Melqart-Hercules here, as well as one of Astarte. There are some fine votive bronzes and terracotta busts in this section, but the most striking objects are two huge anthropoid sarcophagi, one male, one female, carved from marble, and exhibiting strong stylistic influences from both Egypt and Greece. Found nearly a century apart, they both date from around 400 BC and show that, even this late, the city still had important ties with its founders' homeland in the eastern Mediterranean; throughout the ages, trade has been Cádiz's lifeline.

The Roman collection includes some reconstructed burials and displays of grave goods and funerary plaques. There are also some fine sculptures, particularly a large one of the (Andalucían) Emperor Trajan, found at Baelo Claudia.

Upstairs, the art section has some excellent works. From the 15th century is a fine *Virgin Enthroned* by the Flemish Master of Sta Ursula, but the highlight is a fine series of Zurbarán's works from the Carthusian monastery at Jerez. The white-robed saints are painted with the artist's usual expressive treatment of cloth; the fact that he used monks as models make the figures especially realistic. Another

! If you've got problems understanding people here, don't worry, so do Spaniards; the Cádiz accent is widely regarded as the country's most impenetrable.

series of monastery paintings here are by Francisco Osorio, who took on the job when his teacher, Murillo, died. Murillo is, however, represented by a *Stigmata of St Francis*. A portrait of a young Carlos II on horseback is a work by the underrated Asturian court painter Juan Carreño de Miranda; in the European section are two fine Giordanos and a small Rubens *Virgin and Child*. Among more recent works include a portrait by Ignacio Zuloaga, a Miró canvas, and the disturbing *Los Frutos*, by Guillermo Pérez Villalta.

Oratorio de la Santa Cueva
Rosario s/n, **T** 956 222 262. *Tue-Fri 1000-1300, 1630-1930, Sat and Sun 1000-1300, €1.50. Map 1, B7, p251*

Not far from the museum, the Oratorio de la Santa Cueva Rosario is a small chapel attached to the church of El Rosario. The two-tiered chapel, the lower sober neoclassical, the upper more extravagant late Baroque, is of interest for three Goya canvases; serious works depicting the *Loaves and the Fishes*, the *Last Supper*, and the *Wedding Guest*.

Oratorio San Felipe Neri
Calle Santa Inés s/n, south of Plaza San Antonio. *Mon-Sat 1000-1330, €1.20. Map 1, D4, p250*

It was in the Oratorio San Felipe Neri in 1812 that the historic Constitution was proclaimed and the *Cortes* (see p213) were declared in session. The ellipsoid church has two tiers of balconies where the members sat. Plaques on the walls from all over the world commemorate the event, which had an important impact on politics throughout the world. In the *retablo* is a fine *Immaculate Conception* by Murillo.

! During the Civil War, *gaditanos* were such a thorn in the side of the Nationalists that the city was popularly known as *Rusia Chica*.

Museo de las Cortes

Calle Santa Inés s/n, **T** 956 221 788. *Tue-Fri 0900-1300, 1600-1900, Sat and Sun 0900-1300, free. Map 1, D5, p250*

This museum has a large wallpainting of the dramatic events of 1812 (see p213) as well as a staggering 90-sq-m wooden model of the city commissioned by Carlos III in the late 18th century; it's a seriously impressive piece of work by Alfonso Jiménez, an infantry lieutenant.

Near here, it's worth seeking out the sumptuous neo-Moorish **Gran Teatro Falla**, a striking building with striped horseshoe arches. A couple of blocks east of the Oratorio is the **Plaza de las Flores**, officially called the Plaza Topete and full of flower stalls; next to here is the market.

Torre de Tavira

Calle Marqués del Real Tesoro 10, **T** 956 212 910, www.torretavira.com. *Daily 1000-1800 (2000 summer, last entry 30 mins before closing), €3.50. Map 1, D6, p250*

There are great views over the city from this slim, 18th-century tower. Another perspective is given by the fascinating **camera obscura**, a table-top onto which a magnified reflected image of the moving city is projected; it's very intriguing. There's also a small exhibition on the city.

Playa de la Victoria

Map 1, G12, p251

The city's best and biggest beach is Playa de la Victoria, a long strip of clean sand and water in the new part of town. Bus No 1 runs here from the old town every five minutes or so. In summer it's a hive of activity with beach bars and *discotecas*; the streets behind are also full of eating and drinking options.

El Puerto de Santa María

Across the bay from Cádiz, the sherry-producing town of El Puerto de Santa María is but a short boat trip away. It's a favourite spot to head for a seafood lunch on its 'Ribera del Marisco'. There are several notable buildings in this town, which is an important bullfighting centre and home of the late poet Rafael Alberti. In summer, this fairly genteel place changes completely, becoming the focus of some of Andalucía's craziest nightlife.

One of the nicest ways to get to the town is by boat from Cádiz. The old town lies on the west bank of the Río Guadalete, which flows into the Bahía de Cádiz. The town's two beaches are on the bay, Playa de la Puntilla on the city side, and the longer Playa de Valdelagrana on the other side of the river. Several local buses connect the beaches with the old centre.

▸▸ *See Sleeping p100, Eating and drinking p126, Bars and clubs p149*

El Vaporcito, **T** *629 468 014, runs between here and Cádiz and back 5 times a day (6 in summer). The trip takes 40 mins and gives top views of Cádiz on approach. Tickets are €3 single/€5 return. The boat doesn't run on Mon from mid-Sep to mid-May. Last departure from El Puerto is 1730 in winter, and 1930 in summer. There are buses to Cádiz every 30 mins or so (€2.50, 40 mins), leaving from the square outside the bullring. From the same spot are regular departures for Sanlúcar and Chipiona, while from near the train station, buses also go to Jerez hourly or more. El Puerto is on the Cádiz-Jerez cercanía train line and there are frequent services in each direction. There are departures every 30 mins or less, taking 12 mins to Jerez and 35 mins to Cádiz. Sevilla is also frequently served (13 or so a day, 1 hr 20 mins), via Lebrija and Utrera.*

◉ Sights

El Puerto de Santa María wears two hats. Its elegant old town testifies to its days as a burgeoning trading and steamer port – Columbus' 1492 flagship, the *Santa María*, was from here – while its fish restaurants make a popular and hard-to-beat lunch excursion from Cádiz, Jerez or Sevilla. In summer, though, the nearby beach rocks to some of Spain's raunchiest nightlife. El Puerto de Santa María is another sherry town, home to such well-known brands as Osborne and Terry, whose cavernous bodegas impart their distinctive fragrance to the narrow streets.

Castillo de San Marcos
Plaza Alfonso X El Sabio s/n, **T** 956 851 751. *Tue only 1100-1400, free. Map 2, F5, p252*

First constructed by the Moors in the 10th century, the Castillo de San Marcos was rebuilt by Alfonso X in the 13th century, an event he refers to in one of his many writings. Its aspect is formidably attractive, with restored heraldic friezes, dogtooth battlements, and Marian inscriptions decorating the walls and towers. The impressive wooden door only opens one day a week, but it's worth entering to investigate the chapel, built over a mosque, whose foundations it preserves. It also holds a fine Gothic sculpture of *Santa María de España* from the 13th century.

Nuestra Señora de los Milagros
Plaza de España, **T** 956 851 716. *Daily 0830-1200, 1830-2030, free. Map 2, D1, p252*

The Plaza de España Is dominated by Nuestra Señora de los Milagros, a late 15th-century Gothic church with flying buttresses and various 17th-century additions, including the ornate Plateresque/Baroque portal, which has intricate vegetal and cherubic decoration, a tympanum with niches holding sculptures of Mary (standing atop the town's castle) and the Evangelists and, on top of it all, a strange bearded God. The side door is an equally elaborate Gothic affair with curious protruding piers. The sea air isn't helping the limestone, which is severely corroded.

Opposite the church is the ornate façade of the **Museo Municipal** (Calle Pagador 1, **T** 956 542 705, *Tue-Fri 1000-1400, Sat and Sun 1045-1400, free*) once the palace of the Marqués de Candia. It has a mildly diverting collection of archaeological finds and works by local painters.

Fundación Rafael Alberti
Calle Santo Domingo 25, El Puerto de Santa Maria, *T 956 850 711, mid Sep-mid Jun Tue-Sun 1100-1430, rest Mon-Fri 1030-1430 (closed weekends from mid-Jun to mid-Sep), €3. Map 2, F3, p252*

Situated in the house where the 20th-century portuense writer lived as a child, the Fundación Rafael Alberti houses a collection of objects and documents from his life. A Communist and friend of Federico García Lorca, Alberti was one of the important figures of the 'Generación del '27', and most famous for his early collection of poems, *Marinero en tierra* (*Sailor on Land*) and his lyrical autobiography *La arboleda perdida* (*The Lost Grove*). Alberti managed to flee at the end of the Civil War, and stayed in exile until after the death of Franco in 1975.

Plaza de Toros
Plaza Elías Ahuja, **T** 956 541 578. *Tue-Sun 1100-1330, 1730-1900, free, high-quality fights every Sun in Jul and Aug. Map 2, H1, p252*

Looking like a brick Coliseum, the large bullring is one of Spain's more important; indeed an inscription by famous *torero* Joselito claims that if you haven't seen bulls here, you don't know bullfighting. When there's no fight, you can have a look round the ring.

Bodegas

Osborne sherry bodega, **T** 956 869 100. *Open by prior appointment Mon-Fri 1030-1230;* brandy bodega, Ctra NIV Km 651, near the train station, *T 956 854 228. Open by prior appointment Mon-Fri 1030-1330, €4.50.* **Terry**, Calle Toneleros s/n, T 956 857 700. *Mon-Fri 1000-1200, €4.50, prior appointment necessary. Map 2, H2, A2 and A5, p252*

The tourist office will supply a list of the town's wineries that are open for visiting. Most of them require a prior phone call to book. The best known is undoubtedly **Osborne** (a three-syllable word here in Spain) . Founded in the 18th century, the company's 100-odd giant metal black bulls dotted around the country's main roads have become a well-known symbol of Spain. A law forbidding roadside advertising threatened their complete removal in the 1990s (the logo had already been removed for the same reason), but the Supreme Court decreed them to be part of the nation's cultural heritage, so they are here to stay. There are two bodegas in town, one for the sherry, and one for the brandy, which includes the simple but strangely lovable *Magno*.

Another big outfit geared to visits is **Terry**, whose attractive bodega tour includes some fine white Carthusian horses pulling a carriage if there are enough visitors.

Chipiona
Map 6, D3, p257

Chipiona, 9 km south of Sanlúcar, is a cheery seaside town with a marina and fine beaches. It's notable for its lighthouse, whose 344 steps can be climbed for the views. There's a tourist office in the library (Calle Larga 74, *Mon-Fri 0900-1400, 1700-1900, Sat 1100-1330*).

Sanlúcar de Barrameda

In its heyday this delightful Atlantic-facing town was an important port for the Americas and was once even touted as a potential capital of Spain. Its narrow streets still proudly bear the mansions of the town's pomp, and the dukes of Medina Sidonia, descendants of Guzmán El Bueno (of Tarifa fame) still live here. Columbus sailed from here on his third voyage in 1498, and this was the last place Magellan set foot in Spain. In the 19th and 20th centuries it became a fashionable resort and today, some of Andalucía's finest seafood can be eaten in the fishermen's barrio of Bajo de Guía. A happy coincidence this, for Sanlúcar produces arguably Spain's finest accompaniment to fresh shellfish, manzanilla, *a sherry tangy with the taste of the sea breeze. From Sanlúcar you can also take excursions into the avian paradise of Coto Doñana, see p53.*

▸▸ *See Sleeping p101, Eating and drinking p126, Bars and clubs p150*

Linesur runs buses from the station on Av de la Estación. There are hourly buses (currently at 10 past the hr) to Jerez (€1.43, 30 mins) on weekdays, falling to every 2 hrs at weekends. 11 daily buses (5 at weekends) run to Cádiz (€2.55, 1 hr) via El Puerto de Santa María. There are also hourly departures to Chipiona (€0.70, 15 mins) and Sevilla (€6.02, 2 hrs).

◉ Sights

The town is divided into an upper and lower barrio, with most of the action down below, around the central Plaza de Cabildo. On the beach 1 km along from the lower town is Bajo de Guía, location of excellent restaurants. Four kilometres further, the fishing port of **Bonanza** still has a lively afternoon auction in its *lonja*. Sanlúcar is a car trap; there's very little streetside parking, very tight corners and a fiendish one-way system.

The lower town centres on the pretty **Plaza del Cabildo**, surrounded by terraced cafés, and the adjacent **Plaza San Roque**.

From here, you can climb **Calle Bretones**, which passes the lively
food market and **Las Covachas**, a curious Gothic arcade
decorated with sea monsters; its original use is unknown.

Museo del Mar
Calle Truco 4, **T** 956 367 396. *Daily 1000-2200, entry free, donation
appreciated. Map 3, G4, p253*

Continuing up the hill, you get a fine view over the rooftops, one of
which is kitted out as the deck of a ship. This is the eccentric Museo
del Mar, also called Museo de los Caracoles, a private collection of
beachcombed *curios* such as shark jaws (which are for sale, and
over 80,000 seashells. The entrance is just off Plaza San Roque;
you'll be shown around by the owner, who will probably be the
most unusual person you'll meet in Sanlúcar.

Palacio de Orléans-Borbón
Cuesta de Belén s/n, **T** 956 388 000. *Free guided tour of the building
and the theatre Mon, Wed and Fri 1230. Map 3, H3, p253*

Further up the street, passing the very elaborate Teatro Merced,
housed in an old convent, you come to the Palacio de Orléans-
Borbón, a summer palace built by the Duke and Duchess of
Montpensier (the sister of Queen Isabel II of Spain). Now used as
the town hall, it is a fantastic neo-Moorish creation built at the
height of Alhambra romanticism. As well as the stunning porch,
ask the police on duty if you can have a quick peek at the patio.

Nuestra Señora de la O
Plaza de la Paz s/n, **T** 956 361 559. *Open only at 1930, Mass
time. Map 3, H4, p253*

Turning left, you'll come to the church of Nuestra Señora de la O, a
14th-century building with a striking main doorway possessed of

fine *mudéjar* stonework above a Gothic arch. There's delicate blind arching, heraldic lions, and a protruding eave. The round belltower is decorated with paintings of saints; inside, note the star-patterned *mudéjar* ceiling and some 16th-century frescoes.

Palacio de los Duques Medina Sidonia

Plaza Condes de Niebla s/n, **T** 956 360 161. *Tours Sun only 1000-1400, €3. Map 3, H4, p253*

An elegant white building mostly dating from the 19th century, but with some chambers remaining from the 15th-century original. It's still the home of the duchess, a colourful character who is a direct descendant of the Guzmán family who used to rule the town. There's an important archive of historical documents here, as well as numerous works of art and antique furniture. There are also some rooms available to rent.

Further along, the **Castillo de Santiago** is currently closed pending restoration/conversion. Built in the 15th century into part of the city walls, it was here that Fernando and Isabel stayed when they visited the town. Next door is the bodega of Barbadillo, the biggest of the *manzanilla* producers (see below). From the castle, you can descend some steps to the lower town.

Iglesia de Santo Domingo

Calle Ancha, along from Plaza del Cabildo. *Mon-Fri 1000-1200, and around 1900 before Mass; free. Map 3, E6, p253*

The 16th-century Iglesia de Santo Domingo is worth visiting. It has a grand stone arch gateway and a smooth Renaissance façade; the interior is striking too, with elaborate Italianate vaulting under the choir gallery and stately side chapels. Something about the purity of the Renaissance form gives the place a very ancient feel. Keep an eye out for an excellent *Descent from the Cross* by Jacob Jordaens. The *retablos* are Baroque; there's a particularly ornate

★ **Things to do if it happens to rain**

Best

• Museo de Cádiz, Cádiz, p41
• Tour of a *manzanilla* bodega, Sanlúcar de Barrameda, p52
• Centro Andaluz de Flamenco, Jerez de la Frontera, p74
• Monastery of La Rábida, La Rábida, p61
• La Vera Cruz for a long boozy lunch, Vejer de la Frontera, p140

Churrigueresque *Nuestra Señora del Rosario* on the right-hand side, while the large rococo main *retablo* is a work of Pedro de Asensio from the 1760s and is a flourish of vegetal decoration stretching to the ceiling.

Templo de San Francisco

Calle San Nicolás 6, **T** 956 338 800. *Open around 1900 Mon-Sat before Mass. Map 3, E6, p253*

Further along the same street, the Baroque Templo de San Francisco has a colourful dome and bare white interior. The wooden *retablo* is high and elaborate, centred on a sculpture of Mary; the whole is an amazing bit of work, with tendrils seemingly sprouting as you watch. Nearby is a gruesome recumbent Christ with moveable limbs.

Beach

Map 3, B3-A5, p253

The beach is a 10-minute walk from Plaza del Cabildo and is pleasant, with fine, clean sand. It's the scene of a curious spectacle in August, when serious horse races are conducted along it. They have all the trimmings: betting tents, binoculars and prize money (check www.carrerassanlucar.com for dates and details).

Bajo de Guía
Map 3, A5, p253

Turning right along the waterfront, you'll eventually reach Bajo de Guía. This was once the fishermen's quarter and still has a few boats, although the majority of the serious fishing goes on out of nearby Bonanza. There's a string of excellent seafood restaurants here, a fishermen's chapel to **Nuestra Señora del Carmen**, as well as the **Fábrica de Hielo** (**T** 956 381 635, *daily 0900-1900, free*), or former ice factory. It now has a tourist information booth and the booking office for boat trips to the Coto Doñana national park (see below). There's also a display on different zones of the national park, and a good exhibition upstairs on the history of the region and the voyage of Magellan and his crew; there's a model of the only ship from that expedition to make it back: the *Victoria*. The journey took three years and food was, to say the least, scarce: "the biscuit we ate was no longer bread, but powder mixed with maggots which had devoured the substance and had an unbearable odour of being soaked in rats' urine".

The *Real Fernando* is a chunky old boat that runs trips from Sanlúcar across to the Coto Doñana (see p29).

Bodegas
Barbadillo, next to the castle, **T** 956 385 500. *Tours Mon-Sat 1100 (English), 1200 and 1300 (Spanish), €3; Museo de Manzanilla Mon-Sat 1100-1500.* ***Bodegas La Cigarrera***, Plaza Madre de Dios, **T** 956 381 285. *Mon-Sat 1000-1400, €2.50 per person. Map 3, H3 and H6, p253*

There are several *manzanilla bodegas* in town, two of which can be visited without phoning ahead. **Barbadillo** offer slick tours and have upgraded their wine display to the Museo de Manzanilla, detailing all the processes involved from grape to glass. The smaller **Bodegas La Cigarrera** is a more intimate little place.

Coto Doñana

The Huelvan section of the Costa de la Luz has some extraordinary long, sandy beaches, backed by protected dune areas that lead up to the Coto Doñana wetlands. The two towns on the coast, Mazagón and Matalascañas are completely contrasting; the former is a likeably unhurried seaside town with enough employment not to have to rely on tourist traffic. Matalascañas is a large sprawling resort that is packed with partying Sevillanos in summer but depopulated at other times. There are a few campsites and a parador on the beautiful and little-visited strand between the two towns. Although very close to Sanlúcar as the crow flies, to get here requires a long inland journey to cross the Guadalquivir in Sevilla.

▸▸ *See Sleeping p103, Eating and drinking p130, Bars and clubs p151*

 Sights

Mazagón

Buses run from Avenida de la Playa to and from Huelva via Palos. There are 6 a day during the week, falling to 3 on Sat and Sun. 1 bus a day runs to Matalascañas along the coast; there are 2 that make the return trip. These run only on weekdays and are not of use for days at the beach. Map 6, B1, p257

Twenty kilometres east of Huelva, this friendly spot is a fairly low-key place despite its spectacular sandy beach which stretches 10 km east from its marina and centre. Though small, Mazagón bustles year round with seasonal workers from the strawberry plantations and oil refineries to the west, as well as soldiers from the army base nearby. It's one of the best places on the coast off season for this reason, as many of the other beach towns are depressingly lifeless outside the summer months.

The town itself is centred on the Avenida de la Playa, which descends from the main road down to the beach. The further east you head, the better the beach gets; there are several campsites and a parador a few kilometres along from the centre, where the chunky dunes form wooded escarpments backing the strand.

The pedestrian Avenida Fuentepiña has a handful of cheap eateries and cafés. The road east from Mazagón to Matalascañas runs through Mediterranean forest; to the right are the dunes, some of which are substantial cliffs. The bright green of the trees and the pale orange of the sand gives the place an eerie feel in the morning and evening.

Matalascañas

From the bus stop by the tourist office, buses run 7-8 times a day along the length of the town. There are also 7 buses a day to Almonte via El Rocío, 3 a day to Sevilla and 2 a day to Huelva via Palos (none at weekends; change at Almonte for a connection). Map 6, B2, p257

After the quiet charm of Mazagón, the brash development of Matalascañas comes as a shock. Right on the edge of the national park, it's a moderately ugly strip which nevertheless has a long beach of fine-grained sand. In summer, Sevillanos rush here in their thousands to escape the rapidly rising heat levels in the Andalucían capital. In wInter, it's dead.

The Matalascañas beach continues eastwards into the national park itself; you can walk along it, but you can't stray inland. It's a beautiful stretch of sand and you'll see plenty of birdlife; apart from short trails around the visitors' centres, this is the only walking you can actually do within the park boundaries.

At the other end of Matalascañas, near where an old defensive tower, the **Torre Higuera**, is rapidly getting swallowed by the sea, is a complex of migrating dunes, the **Parque Dunar**, not actually part of the national park, but part of its 'buffer zone'. Within this area is the **Museo del Mundo Marino** (Parque Dunar s/n), a modern and interesting display covering all aspects of dune and maritime ecology, particularly focusing on the Bahía de Cádiz area (see p197).

Parque Nacional Coto Doñana

The park cannot be crossed, so there is access from both sides: from Huelva province and from Sanlúcar de Barrameda in Cádiz province (see p48). On the Huelva side are the best installations; four visitors' centres with walking trails along the edge of the park and a number of excellent hides for birdwatching. From here you can also take a 4WD tour into the park itself; this, along with the boat excursion from Sanlúcar, is the only way to actually enter the national park. The best place to base yourself is the town of El Rocío; the tacky resort town of Matalascañas is also close to the centres. With your own transport, you could consider staying in pleasant Mazagón or in one of the duney campsites along the coast. Map 6, B3-C4, p257

The Coto Doñana is one of Europe's most important national parks, a vast area of dunes, wetlands and scrub forest that harbours an incredible array of permanent and migratory birdlife as well as several rare mammals and three distinct botanical zones. For bird-watching, it's a location unparalleled in the peninsula, but anyone with even a passing interest in nature will find it a magical place.

The national park itself covers an area of just over 500 sq km and was initially created in 1969. It's now a UNESCO World Heritage Site and is surrounded by a 'buffer zone', the Parque Natural, which covers a further 542 sq km.

Spring is the best time to visit, as there are huge numbers of breeding birds, unless the winter has been a dry one. Try not to coincide with the Whitsun *romería* to El Rocío (see p58), as all accommodation is booked. In summer, the heat and mosquitoes are intense, but the cooler autumn is also a fine time to be around. Try and book the 4WD tour by phone as far in advance as you possibly can (see below).

The parks are divided into distinct zones. Behind the long sandy beaches is a large area of migratory dunes that move inland; the huge sandhills are interspersed with corrales, gullies wooded with stone pines and Mediterranean shrubs. Beyond here are areas of fixed dunes; these gradually merge into open woodland of cork oak and stone pines, with clearings (*matorrales*) with a great range of scrub. Beyond here are the *marismas*, marshes that are flooded with water in winter and spring by the river Guadalquivir. These are fresh water, being almost completely shielded from the Atlantic by the dune belt and clay soil.

Although the national park itself is heavily protected, nearby development and industry pose a constant threat to the delicate natural balance of the area. No sooner does one proposal for a block of tourist apartments or a golf course (whose irrigation needs are a dangerous threat) get quashed by environmental lobbying that another takes its place. While the creation of the *parque natural* has helped matters, you only need look at burgeoning Matalascañas right alongside the national park to realize that things are far from secure. Many locals feel strongly that the park hinders jobs and profits from new construction, while the very limited access gives few tourist euros back to the community in compensation. While current restrictions on visits are ideal for the ducks and lynxes, they don't vote, so environmental activists are constantly vigilant lest the government approves something that could cause lasting damage. In 1998, when a huge flow of toxic waste from a burst reservoir was stopped just outside the Doñana wetlands, wildlife was severely impacted; fortunately it is recovering well.

Visitors' centres

The principal visitors' centre is at **El Acebuche** (11.5 km off the Matalascañas-El Rocío road, **T** 959 448 711, *daily 0800-1900, 2100 in summer*), an essential stop if you are interested in what the region has to offer. Passing buses will drop you at the turn-off on request and are surprisingly good at looking out for people waiting to return. Situated by a lake, the centre has two circular walks (1.5 km and 3.5 km) and several peaceful thatched observatories. The centre itself appropriately has a huge storks' nest on the roof. The hides have informative panels on the birdlife, but don't have telescopes, so bring binoculars if you have some. You'll easily see coots, moorhens, purple gallinules and a range of duck species.

From the El Acebuche centre you can book 4WD bus tours of the park; this is the only way you can visit the national park itself apart from peeking in at the edges. The tours are enjoyable, but serious nature fans may get annoyed at the chattering tourists and limited viewing time available. Take your own binoculars if at all possible; otherwise be sure to hire a pair from the visitors' centre before departing.

Two other visitors' centres, **Palacio del Acebrón** and **La Rocina**, both daily 0900-1900 (2100 in summer), are close together and within a short walk of El Rocío township. La Rocina has a hut with an exhibition on the pilgrimage, an audiovisual display on the wildlife of the area and a 3.5-km trail that runs along the edge of the wetlands; there are five good hides here. From Palacio del Acebrón, 5 km beyond La Rocina, is a short woodland trail with some viewpoints.

Another centre, **José Antonio Valverde**, is some 50-km drive from El Rocío via Villamanrique de la Condesa. On the edge of the wetlands, it's one of the best and most isolated spots for observing the birds of the park. However, it's tricky to get to if you don't have your own transport.

On the southeastern side of the national park, there's one other visitors' centre; from here you can take a boat tour into the national park. These leave from Sanlúcar de Barrameda (see p48).

Flora and fauna
The protected conditions and different ecosystems here make it a paradise of wildlife. Along the beaches, seabirds and coastal birds thrive; including sandwich terns, oystercatchers, scoters, cormorants, sanderlings and Kentish plover. Turtles and, offshore, whales are also sometimes seen. The dunes are home to small rodents and stands of stone pine, while the woodlands beyond are of lentisks, stone pine and cork trees interspersed with cistus, gorse, lavender and rosemary. This area harbours several larger

mammals; herds of fallow and roe deer, genets, wild boar and the rare Pardel lynx, a nocturnal beast that is a very rare sighting. While the wild camels, originally brought by the Moors, have died out (poached for the pot), there are also wild cows and horses, as well as mongoose, polecats and, in the *marismas*, otters. The wetlands are home or stopover to hundreds of species of birds. Wading birds include white storks, spoonbills, egrets, avocets, stilt, godwit, lapwing and several species of heron. Ducks, coots, moorhens and the park's emblem, the purple gallinule, are present in huge numbers, while wintering greylag geese arrive in their tens of thousands. In the reeds and scrub are nightingales, hoopoe, partridge, bee-eaters and azure-winged magpies, as well as Cettis warblers and great reed-warblers. Birds of prey abound, the rare imperial eagle, as well as booted eagles, short-toed eagles, buzzards, harriers and three types of kite. The best spots to see birds are the bridge and walkway at El Rocío and the hides and paths of the visitor centres.

El Rocío

Tourist office, **T** 959 443 808, *on the main road, just north of the turn-off to the church. There are 3 daily buses to and from Sevilla (€6.50, 1 hr 30 mins); these run on to Matalascañas. 5 additional buses ply the Almonte-Matalascañas route; you'll have to change at 1 of these towns to reach Huelva, but connections are fairly good. All these buses will stop at the El Acebuche and Las Rocinas visitors' centres on request. Map 6, B3, p257*

Famous throughout the country, this village is the climax of the boisterous Whitsun pilgrimage (see box, p59) to adore its famous Virgin. As well as perching on the edge of the Doñana wetlands, it's a striking place. With all its bumpy roads of rutted sand and earth, half its inhabitants seemingly on horseback and its houses built of wooden planks with horse-hitches outside, it looks like a film set from a spaghetti western. Though the town has a small population,

Pilgrimage of the White Dove

The Whitsun *romería* to the Huelvan village of El Rocío is the most colourful, boisterous and well-attended of Spain's many pilgrimages. Nearly a million people descend on the Wild West-like town for the weekend before Pentecost Monday, many arriving on foot and in oxcarts as part of *cofradías* (brotherhoods) from all over Andalucía, each with their own processional float, or *simpecado*, with an image of the Virgin. Many men and women wear traditional *corto* and flamenca costumes and the atmosphere is a strange mixture of religious solemnity, horsemanship, social bonding and drunken abandonment. On the journey to El Rocío, *rocieras* (flamenco-style songs about the pilgrimage), wine, food and sex meld around the campfires.

The object of the pilgrimage is the Virgen del Rocío (Virgin of the Dew), a 13th-century sculpture housed in a modern sanctuary. The town fills way beyond capacity over the Whitsun weekend and little

sleeping goes on between the open-air masses, impromptu fiestas, galloping horses and competitive *cofradía* rivalries.

On the Sunday night, the Virgin, popularly known as the *Blanca Paloma* (White Dove) leaves her sanctuary and visits the chapels of all the *cofradías*, who aggressively jostle for the honour of carrying her part of the way. "Viva la Paloma Blanca" is the cry reverberating through the sandy streets of the wetland town.

The *romería* is often described as typifying Andalucía in its mixture of pride, emotion, hedonism and sentimentality and is an unforgettable experience that creates lifelong friends and draws people back year after year.

Whitsunday falls on 15 May 2005, 4 June 2006, 27 May 2007 and 11 May 2008. There's also a smaller Rocío on 19 August.

Every seven years the Virgin is dressed as a shepherdess and carried reverently into the hills, there to spend nine months before returning to her sanctuary.

it's a sizeable place, due to the fact that all the pilgrimage brotherhoods maintain chapels and lodgings here. El Rocío is a characterful base to explore the Doñana Park and is particularly worth visiting at weekends, when it's always cheerfully busy with families dropping in on the Virgin, folk doing a spot of birdwatching or brotherhoods engaged in DIY repairs to their premises.

The centre of attention is the **Ermita del Rocío** (*daily 0830-2000, free*), home of the Virgin that inspires the pilgrimage and a whole genre of Andalucían music – *rocieras*. A shiny white structure built between 1964 and 1969, it has weathered a fair bit of criticism for being over grand, but in reality is fairly simple and doesn't pull focus from the Virgin herself. The same can't be said for the ugly *retablo* she is housed in. The sculpture itself is a work from the 13th century, a pale full-faced beauty dressed elaborately and with the appearance of being hooded. There's normally a torrent of flowers at her feet. An exterior chamber chokes with the smoke of the thousands of votive candles lit every week; it is difficult to over-emphasize just how important La Blanca Paloma is to Andalucíans. Souvenir stalls thrive all around, selling pictures of the Virgin with messages for world peace alongside toy guns to keep the kids amused. No photos are allowed in the church, for purely commercial reasons.

Right across from the church is the beginning of the Coto Doñana National Park, here in the form of year-round wetlands fed by the Río Madre de las Marismas. There are substantial populations of deer and semi-wild horses; needless to say, there's excellent bird (and mosquito) life. Following the water to your left, past the Hotel Toruño, you'll reach an observation centre (*Tue-Sun 1000-1400, 1600-1900, free*); in the evenings here you can observe an array of avians and there are helpful staff on duty. The road bridge across the water is also an excellent place for nature-watching.

The area around the church and alongside the marismas is studded with *acebuche* (wild olive) trees, some of which are well over half a millennium old.

Lugares Colombinos

Just a few kilometres north of Mazagón, on the estuary of the Río Tinto, are the so-called Lugares Colombinos, a group of sites which are intimately connected with the voyages of Cristóbal Colón (Christopher Columbus).

 ## Sights

La Rábida

T *959 350 411, Tue-Sat 1000-1300, 1600-1900 (1600-1815 Oct-Mar, 1100-1300, 1700-1900 Jul and Aug), Sun 1045-1300, €2.50/€3 includes audio guide in several languages. Park a little bit away from the monastery itself to avoid incurring a €1 fee. Map 6, A1, p257*

Within a large botanical park directly across the river from Huelva, the monastery of La Rábida was where Columbus struggled and schemed with two of the monks for ways to win the support of Fernando and Isabel, the Catholic monarchs, for his project. He first arrived here with his son Diego in 1484, after João II of Portugal had refused to sponsor his voyage. He was attracted here for several reasons: one of the Franciscans, Fray Antonio de Marchena, knew Isabel; the area was also full of mariners with a deep knowledge of the Atlantic and its secrets.

The 14th-century monastery has been much altered over the years, but several parts remain much as they were when Columbus stayed here. On entry, the first cloister is decorated with intriguing modern paintings by Juan Manuel Núñez depicting part of the Columbus story. Off here is the stunning chapel, entered through a horseshoe arch: the building was once an Almohad fortress. On the walls are half-preserved 15th-century frescoes, while above the main altar is a replica of the early Gothic crucifixion that hung here until its destruction in the Civil War. Luckily the same fate didn't befall the Virgen de la Rábida, a small late 13th-century alabaster Mary in a small chapel opposite the door. She wears a crown placed on her by the Pope during the 500-year celebrations of Columbus' voyage. It seems certain that Columbus and his crew would have prayed here before setting out, and the chapel is one of the spots that most evokes the explorer's memory. The ceiling is a fine neo-*mudéjar artesonado*.

The second cloister is striking; an ensemble of brick *mudéjar* arches with a whitewashed upper level. Off it are a small meeting-room where Columbus probably discussed strategies for royal approval with the abbot Juan Pérez, and the refectory, which has been effectively returned to approximately its original state. In the former is a small portrait of Columbus by the artist Valeriano Bécquer, brother of the famous poet Gustavo Adolfo. Upstairs is the chapterhouse, where final planning for the voyages took place. Even after gaining royal approval, it was tough for the foreigner Columbus to persuade skeptical local mariners to come along on the voyage. Alonso Pinzón, an experienced captain from Palos, was brought on board (so to speak), and he managed to put together a crew.

Also upstairs is an exhibition, with models of the ships, facsimile documents (including several examples of Columbus' mysterious signature) and samples of soil from the Philippines and from all the countries of the Americas. One of the items on display is the sword of Hernan Cortés' principal captain, Sandoval. Cortés and Pizarro both came here in the course of planning their journeys.

Muelle de las Carabelas

T 959 530 597, *mid-Sep to Easter Tue-Sun 1000-1900, Easter to mid-Sep Tue-Fri 1000-1400, 1700-2100, Sat and Sun 1100-2000,* €3. *Map 6, A1, p257*

Below the monastery, on the water, are replicas of the three ships from the 1492 voyage moored by an exhibition centre. The ships are unadorned and remarkable mainly for their tiny size. The *Santa María* is in the middle; using a larger, more traditional hull, she proved too unwieldy and was eventually wrecked off Hispaniola.

The voyages of Columbus

Christopher Columbus (Cristóbal Colón in Spanish) was probably born near Genoa in 1451. Little is known of his early life, but he made his way to Portugal, Britain and then Madeira, where he married in 1480 and became interested in the popular idea of sailing westwards to Asia.

Rejected by João II of Portugal, he travelled to Spain and petitioned Fernando and Isabel who eventually agreed to furnish him with three ships and letters to take to the Great Khan on her behalf. On 3 August 1492, Columbus left Palos de la Frontera with three small ships, *La Pinta*, *La Niña* and *La Santa María*, and on 12 October they reached the Bahamas, which they named San Salvador. The expedition then discovered Cuba and Hispaniola, establishing a fort, Navidad, on the latter.

Columbus arrived back in Spain on 15 March to great excitement and honour. He brought with him exotic fruits and cereals, as well as six bewildered native Americans.

His second voyage began later the same year, this time equipped with 17 ships and over 1,000 men to establish settlements. He discovered several more Caribbean islands, including Puerto Rico and Jamaica, and founded a permanent settlement on Hispaniola. On his third voyage (1498-1500), he made landfall on the South American coast, in modern-day Venezuela, but things turned sour when his heavy-handed governorship of the Hispaniola colony led to a revolt. The Spanish government had him imprisoned and sent home; he was received well, but lost his position as governor of the New World Colonies.

On his final voyage (1502-04) Columbus reached the Central American isthmus, exploring the coast from Honduras down to Panama. He still believed, against most learned opinion, that he had discovered outlying parts of Asia. He died in Valladolid in 1506, temporarily at least, a forgotten man.

The smaller caravelles (*Niña* on the left, *Pinta* on the right) moved better with the swells and didn't take so much damage in high seas. Walking around the dock, there's an unbelievably patronizing display of plastic native Americans, complete with taped soundtrack of screeching parrots. A shamefully tokenistic display of South American craft is upstairs in the building, which also contains a more comprehensive exhibition on the voyages.

Also within the park is a large amphitheatre, which, to the council's credit, does make an effort to bring over performance groups from Africa and South America during the summer months. There's also a large monument to *Faith and Exploration*, as well as a smaller one to *Plus Ultra*, the first plane to make it across the Atlantic. Unfortunately, the peaceful hotel by the monastery now only caters to groups. The park itself has many plant species from different areas of the American continent.

Palos de la Frontera
Map 6, A1, p257

This small town was once a heartland of hardened Atlantic mariners but has now been left high and dry as the estuary has silted up. Columbus embarked on his first expedition from here, and the three ships were at least a quarter crewed by Palos men. Palos was the home of the Pinzón brothers who did much of the organizing and captained two of the ships that the port had been ordered to provide for him by royal decree.

Nowadays Palos is a small pleasant Spanish country town devoted to strawberry-farming and basically consisting of one long street that rises to the centre and then drops away to where the port used to be. The central square is named Plaza Franco, not after the dictator, but rather his brother, who flew from Palos to Buenos Aires in 1926, thus becoming the first person to cross the Atlantic by plane. Up the hill from here is the **house of Martín Alonso**

1 *Vejer de la Frontera has a very Moorish feel to it: narrow, dazzling white streets and flower-filled patios .* ▶▶ *See page 86.*

2 *Cádiz Carnival celebrations last for nine days and are very different to those of the rest of the peninsula.* ▶▶ *See page 168.*

3 *The most enjoyable way to eat tapas is to visit several bars, having a drink and trying the different specialities in each one.* ▶▶*See page 120.*

4 *Britain is still the world's biggest consumer of sherry and there's a distinctly British air to the region's winemaking culture.* ▶▶ *See page 70.*

5 *A purple gallinule in the Cota Donana National Park. This vast area of dunes, wetlands and scrub forest provides the best birdwatching in Spain.* ▶▶ *See page 55.*

6 *Arcos de la Frontera has a dramatic hilltop position, with many buildings worriedly peering over the edge of the crumbly cliffs.* ▶▶*See page 78.*

Ascot on the Strand
If you fancy a day at the races, head for the beach at Sanlúcar de Barrameda in August.

Wet and wild
As well as birds, the Cota Doñana wetlands are home to wild cows, mongooses, polecats and otters.

Sea, sand and sailboards
South of Cádiz there are uncrowded beaches backed by rolling pastures and green hills.

Fruits of the sea
In Sanlúcar de Barrameda you can accompany some of Andalucía's finest seafood with a tangy manzanilla sherry.

Die Another Day
*The latest Bond film wasn't shot in Havana at all,
but in the elegant streets of Cádiz's old town.*

Up, up on a wave
The winds of Tarifa have made it a kitesurfing hotspot.

Frenetic and flirtatious
Flamenco culture is alive and well in Jerez de la Frontera.

Pinzón, captain of the *Pinta* and Columbus' right hand in the organization of the voyage. It's been restored as a museum (Calle Cristóbal Colón 24, *Mon-Fri 1030-1330, 1700-1930; closed for restoration but due to reopen in 2005*), which includes information about Franco's flight as well as Columbus' first expedition.

Further along the main road is the **Iglesia de San Jorge** (*Tue-Fri 1000-1200, 1800-2000*), which once stood directly above the wharf where Columbus embarked. He surely prayed here before setting sail; an inscription on the church's wall proclaims Palos' pride in its connection with the voyage: *Oh Palos, no puede tu gloria igualar ni Menfis ni Tebes ni Roma inmortal* (Oh Palos, your glory cannot be equalled by Memphis, nor Thebes, nor immortal Rome). The church is heavily laden with storks and has an attractive interior, including a fine Gothic alabaster sculpture of Santa Ana and some colourful frescoes. Built in the 15th century, it is the characteristic Andalucían mix of the Gothic and the *mudéjar*. Below the church is a small brick fount; it is said that the ships took on their water supply from here before setting sail.

Moguer

Tourist office, in the grounds of the ruined castle, **T** *959 371 850, Mon-Fri 1030-1330, 1700-1900 (1800-2000 summer), will provide you with a town map. Some buses will drop you off nearby on Avenida América, and there's a free car park right outside the castle. Map 6, A1, p257*

Although the *Niña* was built here, the town provided several of the crew for Columbus' first voyage, and the mariner visited the town several times, Moguer perhaps owes more of its fame to its Nobel prize-winning poet Juan Ramón Jiménez (1881-1958), who deeply loved his home despite having to spend the last 20 years of his life across the Atlantic once Franco came to power. A particularly attractive, if not effusively welcoming town, whitewashed Moguer is worth exploring both for its several fine monuments and sites relevant to the life of Juan Ramón. Quotes from the poet's best-known work, *Platero y yo*, are tiled up around the town in various locations. The book is a lyrical portrait of the town and the region conducted as a conversation between the writer and his donkey, Platero, with whom Jiménez used to wander the town's streets, and who is buried in the grounds of the Casa Fuentepiña, a private residence to the south of town where the poet spent his summers writing.

The ruined castle has origins as a Roman tower but was basically built by the Almohads, before being enlarged by the Castillian monarchs.

The **Ayuntamiento** (town hall) is on Plaza del Cabildo, near the tourist office. So harmonious is its late-Baroque façade with two levels of round arches on marble columns that it used to feature on the 2,000 peseta note; you can still watch Spanish visitors start as they try to work out where they've seen the building before.

Beyond the plaza, down Calle Reyes Católicos, you soon come to the huge parish church, **Santa María de Granada**. It is strikingly Sevillian in style with its yellow and blue tiling and a belltower whose design is clearly based on the Giralda, although on a smaller scale. The church can only be visited before evening mass (doors open around 1900); the statue of the Virgin is in pride of place under a well-proportioned *baldacchino*.

Returning to **Plaza del Cabildo**, head up the pleasing pedestrian street of Calle Andalucía past the elegant public library, then past a small Renaissance chapel that once belonged to a Franciscan monastery. Next to the chapel, where the monastery's entrance once was, is the exuberant tiled façade of the **Teatro Felipe Godínez**.

Further up this street you reach the *Convento de San Francisco*, now home to the provincial archive. It's a blend of the *mudéjar* and the mannerist Baroque; its cobbled cloister and spire belong to the latter, while the austere single-naved church itself is mostly memorable *mudéjar* brick, although heavily restored after earthquake damage. The main *retablo* is a fine example of 18th-century Spanish Baroque. This monastery was an important training centre for missionary monks, who then embarked for the Americas.

Moguer's finest building is just around the corner; the **Monasterio de Santa Clara** (**T** 959 370 107, *Tue-Sat by guided tour at 1100, 1200, 1300, 1700, 1800, 1900, €1.80*). Founded in the 14th century, it presents a distinctly fortified appearance with its sturdy buttresses, particularly from Plaza de las Monjas, from which it is separated by a low castellated wall. The visit takes you through a pretty *mudéjar* cloister, then a larger Renaissance one, filled with palms and bananas brought back from the New World. After passing through the rooms of the daily lives of the nuns, who were here until the 1950s, you enter the church, the highlight of which is the fine carved marble tombs of the Portocarrero family, and the alabaster ones of the founding Tenorio family. A plaque commemorates the fact that Columbus spent a whole night here praying on his return to Palos; something he had promised to the Virgin if she delivered his ships from a terrible Atlantic storm that threatened to send the expedition to the bottom. Note also the choir stalls, excellent *mudéjar* work influenced from the art of Nasrid Granada.

Two of Juan Ramón Jiménez's houses are open to the public. His birthplace, the **Casa Natal** (Calle Ribera 2, north of the Convento de Santa Clara, **T** 959 372 148, *Tue-Sat 1015-1315, 1715-1915, Sun 1015-1315*), with wrought-iron balconies so typical of the town, has been restored to what it would have looked like, and contains various curios of the poet's childhood. The **Casa Museo Zenobia y Juan Ramón** (Calle Juan Ramón Jiménez 10, **T** 959 372 148, *Tue-Sat 1000-1400, 1700-2000, Sun 1000-1400, €1.80*), where he lived with his beloved wife Zenobia. This typical Andalucían patioed house has a more comprehensive collection of documents and folios, including the notification by telegram of the Nobel Prize for Literature in 1956. Both houses were closed for restoration at the time of writing; ring ahead. The couple are buried in the town cemetery to the east of town in an ornate monument.

Jerez de la Frontera

Quiet, genteel Jerez is quite a contrast to nearby Cádiz. Actually larger than its provincial capital, it rarely feels like it. The city is famous for its sherry, the wine that takes its name from the place and known in Falstaff's day as 'sack' (see box, p70). Over the centuries the British, largest overseas consumers of the stuff, have had a strong connection with the city and its wine industry, and some of their customs have rubbed off on the locals – corduroy elbow patches aren't a common sight elsewhere in the country. Jerez is also known as an important centre of flamenco and of horsemanship – the dancing white Carthusian mounts have a training base here (see box p74). Jerez is also venue for the Spanish motorcycling Grand Prix, which normally takes place around the time of its May feria, a fine time to be in town if you can find accommodation.

Jerez is derided by other cities in Andalucía as being pijo (posh), but the same gentle politeness that causes the comment makes it, as a place to visit, helpful and hospitable.

▸▸ *See Sleeping p106, Eating and drinking p133, Bars and clubs p152*

Jerez is easily reached by public transport from either Sevilla or Cádiz. The train and bus stations are adjacent at the eastern end of town, a 15-min walk from the centre. Jerez's airport is 8 km northeast and has weekend Ryanair flights to and from London Stansted, as well as connections to Madrid and Barcelona. For further details, see Transport, p19. Local bus No 10 runs from the train and bus stations into town. There are no buses to the airport, but a taxi will only cost around €10. Most of Jerez's sights are within walking distance of the centre, but for the further flung ones jump on a local bus in the Plaza del Arenal; you can't miss them as they're a sickly mauve colour. The tourist office has a route map. Visiting during the Feria de Caballo, Jerez's main fiesta in the first half of May, is recommended, but you'll struggle to find

accommodation. Many revellers just come down from Sevilla or
train and stay up. Jerez gets very hot in summer, so spring and
autumn are the most suitable times for a visit.

◉ Sights

The centre of Jerez is the elegant **Plaza del Arenal**, whose
southern end is covered with the tables of poor-quality tourist
restaurants. Many of the city's principal sights, as well as several
of its best tapas bars, are within a short distance of here.

Alcázar
Alameda Vieja s/n, **T** *956 319 798. Daily 1000-1800 winter,*
1000-2000 summer (except Jun-Sep when it shuts at 1500 on Sun),
€1.50, €3.30 including camera obscura, which has shows every ½
hr until 30 mins before closing. Map 4, H4, p254

The Alcázar complex has a bit of everything. A sturdy fortress
built by the Almohads, it was a sometime residence of the
Seville kings of that period. It preserves some atmospheric
Arab baths as well as the interesting church of Santa María
la Real, which retains many of the features from its days as
a mosque, including the *mihrab*. The Palacio de Villavicencio
is a mostly 18th-century structure which houses a **camera
obscura** giving views over the city and as far as the coast.
The Alcázar's gardens are particularly well maintained and try
to give a Moorish ambience.

> **!** "If I had a thousand sons, the first humane principle I would
> teach them should be, to forswear thin potations and to
> addict themselves to sack."
> (W Shakespeare, Henry IV Part II)

Of sherry and other Andalucían nobles

James Bond: Pity about your liver, sir. Unusually fine *Solera*. '51, I believe.

M: There is no year for sherry, 007. (*Diamonds Are Forever*)

Sherry wines are produced in the area around Jerez de la Frontera, from which their English name derives. The region has a long winemaking history; the wines of Jerez were popular in Britain long before Shakespeare wrote about Falstaff putting away quarts of 'sack' to drown his sorrows or keep out the cold. The country is still the biggest consumer and there's a distinctly British air to the region's winemaking culture.

The two principal grapes used for the production of sherry wines are the white Palomino Fino (the majority) and Pedro Ximénez. The region's soils have a massive influence on the final product; the chalky *albariza* tends to produce the finest grapes. Palomino produces the best dry wines, while Pedro Ximénez tends to be dried in the sun before pressing, optimizing its sugar levels for a sweeter wine.

There are two principal styles of sherry, but no decision is taken on which will be produced from each cask's contents until a couple of months after the vintage. This decision is taken by the *capataz* (head cellarperson), who tastes the wines, which are poured using the distinctive long-handled *venencia*, designed so as not to disturb the yeast on the wine's surface. Those destined to become rich, nutty *olorosos* are fortified to about 18% to prevent yeast growth; these wines are destined for aging and may later be sweetened and coloured to produce styles such as cream or *amoroso*. The best *olorosos* may be aged 25 years or more. *Finos*, on the other hand, are fortified to a lower level and nurtured so as to optimize the growth of the naturally occurring local yeast, *flor*. This produces a pale, dry wine, with a very distinctive clean finish, a perfect tapas accompaniment.

Manzanillas are *finos* that have been aged in the seaside environment of Sanlúcar de Barrameda; the salty tang is perceptible. Gallons of *manzanilla* are drunk during the Sevilla Feria, and *manzanilla* sales have just outstripped sales of regular *fino* for the first time in Spain. *Amontillados* are *finos* aged longer than normal so that some oxidation occurs after the protective layer of yeast has died away. Some of these are sweetened for the British market.

Another curiosity of sherry production is the use of the *solera*. This is a system of connected barrels designed to ensure the wine produced is consistent from one year to the next. The wine is bottled from the oldest barrels (butts),

which are in turn refilled from the next oldest, until the last are filled with the new wine. While the wine produced has no vintage date, the age of the *solera* is a matter of pride, and there are many around that are well over a century old. The butts themselves are sometimes used for up to a hundred years.

Other similar Andalucían wines are *Montilla*, from Córdoba province. Much like a sherry in style, the difference lies in the fact that they are rarely fortified. *Málaga* wines are fortified and mainly sweet; those from the highest grade, *lágrima*, are pressed using only the weight of the grapes and can be very good indeed.

Brandy is also made in Jerez. Although conoisseurs of French brandies usually sniff at the oaky nature of these *Marlons*, there are some good ones produced, and even the cheaper varieties are rarely bad. The spirit is produced using sherry casks, and the same *solera* system is employed.

La Catedral

Plaza de la Catedral s/n, **T** 956 319 798. *Mon-Fri 1100-1300, 1800-2000, Sat and Sun 1100-1300, free. Map 4, G4, p254*

Across the way, Jerez's cathedral is built over the old main mosque. Often dismissed by guidebooks, it's an interesting structure. Although mostly built in the 18th century, it has clear Gothic pretensions with flying buttresses and sculpted pinnacles, as well as Renaissance features. To one side stands the belltower, an exceptionally elegant 15th-century *mudéjar* creation with delicate blind arching and a slender form; it belonged to the previous church. The main portal is a triple doorway crowned with scenes of the *Immaculate Conception*, the *Nativity* and the *Adoration*. The five-naved interior feels less Gothic and has elaborate vaulting, a high, narrow dome and a curious stripy effect with the white cement having been deliberately bled over the grey stone a little. There are high stained-glass windows of saints along the central nave, and a fine Zurbarán *Madonna and Child*, but little else of great artistic merit.

Iglesia de San Miguel

Map 4, H6, p254

The Iglesia de San Miguel is the most interesting of Jerez's churches. Situated a short way south of Plaza del Arenal, it is immediately noticeable for its ornate 17th-century belltower, which unusually stands right above the middle of the main entrance, an ornate, geometrically decorated façade. Around to the left is the original main door, an Isabelline portal with elaborate Gothic pinnacles. Inside, the main *retablo* is a masterpiece by Juan Martínez Montañés.

Nearby, on Calle Ramón de Cala, have a look at the powerful monument to the flamenco singer and dancer Lola Flores, a recent creation by one of Spain's top modern sculptors, Víctor Ochoa, standing in front of an elegant orange *palacio*.

Plaza de Asunción
Map 4, F5, p254

Near the cathedral, the Plaza de Asunción is a beautiful square with two proud buildings on it: one is the 15th-century church of San Dionisio with yet another *mudéjar* belltower, while the other is the former town hall, with a superbly carved Plateresque façade and curious loggia with two rows of arches.

Barrio de Santiago
Map 4, D3, p254

North of Plaza de Asunción stretch the narrow streets of the oldest part of the town, part of which is the barrio of Santiago. One of the curious things about Jerez is that alongside its well-heeled sherry population is a large gypsy community whose flamenco almost rivals the wine in quality and fame. Santiago is the centre of the gypsy population and is a good spot for a wander, with several interesting churches and a couple of museums. Of the former, San Mateo is worth a visit primarily for its staggeringly elaborate Baroque *retablo*.

Museo Arqueológico
Plaza Mercado s/n, **T** 956 333 316. *Tue-Sun 1000-1400, 1600-1900, €1.70. Map 4, E2, p254*

Although not a patch on the one in Cádiz, Jerez's archaeological museum is very attractive, with its collection laid out around a light patio as well as darker, atmospherically lit chambers. The ground floor is devoted to prehistory, while the first floor has some fine Roman portrait heads, funerary plaques and amphorae as well as the collection's showpiece, a bronze Greek military helmet from the 17th century BC. Upstairs is a Moorish and medieval collection as well as a café with a terrace.

▶ **Fancy horses**

In Moorish times, there were two basic types of horses in the peninsula: the heavy, northern mount, originally brought by the Celts and of Germanic bloodlines, and the lighter *berberisco* horses of the south, elegant beasts suitable for light cavalry. These were originally brought across from North Africa but were resident in the peninsula well before the Moors' arrival. After the Reconquest, the Castillian crown wished to merge the two species to create an all-purpose 'Spanish' horse. This duly happened, but a few landowners refused to surrender their pure Andalucían horses and gave them into the care of Carthusian monks, who maintained a breeding program of the elegant creatures that some say are descended from the unicorn, as a bony protrusion on the muzzle is a common genetic trait. Thus the horses came to be known as Carthusians, or *Cartujanos*, and have been very highly prized ever since for their beauty and grace.

Although the monasteries were disentailed in the 1830s, a few breeders kept the line going. They are often fastidiously groomed and dressed and highly trained to 'dance' or walk sideways, a spectacle you can see at *corridas de rejones*, the horseback bullfights, or at the Real Escuela de Arte Ecuestre in Jerez, the city traditionally linked with the noble beasts.

Centro Andaluz de Flamenco

Plaza San Juan 1, **T** 956 349 265. *Mon-Fri 1000-1400, free.*
Map 4, D3, p254

This important centre holds a large archive of printed music, recordings and videos of flamenco; it's the country's principal body for the promotion of the art. As well as various temporary exhibitions, screenings of performances by some of the art's greatest names are shown daily; you can also request videos or cassettes from the archive. The centre is also a good source of information about upcoming events and performances.

Real Escuela Andaluza de Arte Ecuestre
Avenida Duque de Abrantes s/n, **T** 956 319 635, reservas@real escuela.org. *Show every Thu at midday, also on Tue at the same time Mar-Oct. Training sessions 1000-1300 weekdays when there's no show. Show €17, training sessions €6. Map 4, A6, p254*

This training centre for the white Carthusian horses is a popular drawcard. There's a weekly show (twice weekly in the summer) where the elegant dancing beasts sashay around to symphony music, with riders dressed in traditional costume. Dubbed an 'equestrian ballet', it really is quite astounding. It can be equally enjoyable to attend the morning training sessions and watch horse and rider develop the necessarily close relationship required to perform such complex movements; at these times you can also visit the stables.

Centro Temático La Atalaya
Calle Cervantes 3, **T** 956 182 100. *Entry in groups by time slot. **Palacio del Tiempo**, Tue-Sat 1000-1400, 1700-1800, €5.10. **Misterio de Jerez**, Tue-Sat 1100-1300, and 1800, €6. In summer both are open Tue-Sun 1000-1900. Combined ticket €9. Map 4, A4, p254*

This new complex combines two museums. Jerez's much-loved collection of clocks and watches has been given a contemporary slant and renamed the **Palacio del Tiempo** (Palace of Time). It's an absorbing collection of pieces from all over the world that now takes the form of a 'voyage through time'. Next to it is the **Misterio de Jerez**, a museum devoted to the sherry industry, with numerous fancy special effects that don't quite justify the entrance prices.

Bodegas

González Byass, Calle Manuel María González 12,
T 956 357 016, reservas@gonzalezbyass.es. *Regular tours in English Mon-Sat 1130, 1330, 1400, 1530, 1730, Sun 1130, 1330, 1400; Spanish hourly, also French, and German; €7.50, or €11.50 for the 1400 visit which throws in some tapas. Map 4, H3, p254*
Pedro Domecq, Calle San Ildefonso 3, **T** 956 151 500, **F** 956 338 764, *Mon-Fri 1000-1300, €5, children under 16 free. Map 4, F2, p254* **Sandeman**, Calle Pizarro 10, **T** 956 151 711. *Map 4, A4, p254*

Most of sherry's big names have their bodegas here: Domecq, González Byass, Sandeman, Garvey and many more. Most of the bodegas can be visited, although many require a phone call the day before to arrange it. This is worth the effort and rarely a problem; if you're lucky you'll get a very personal tour.

The two most-visited of the bodegas don't require a booking and both are handily near the cathedral. The most famous sherry is Tío Pepe, the high-grade *fino* of the **González Byass** company, the biggest of Jerez's producers. Their massive complex can be visited on a slick, slightly Disneyfied tour. You'll learn nothing about the sherry-making process but will have a pleasant ride around the pretty bodega in a small train. Highlights include a pavilion designed by Gustave Eiffel, drunken mice, barrels signed by all manner of celebrities who have visited, and a tasting room left in original early-19th-century state. Although the tour is pricey, there's a generous tasting session at the end of it.

Just up the hill from the cathedral, **Pedro Domecq** is a good bodega to visit. The tour is more informative than González Byass and more personal. Staff will happily give explanations in English alongside the Spanish. The tour takes in both the sherry and brandy ageing areas, and has a glass-ended barrel so you can see the thick flor yeast. There are signed barrels here too, including one by Franco. When King Alfonso XIII visited the bodega, the Domecq family considered it a discourtesy to make him cross a public street to get from one part of the complex to another. The solution: they bought the street, a typical piece of sherry-baron thinking. The tasting here is exceptionally generous and includes two brandies, one of which, *Fundador*, was Hemingway's standard tipple when in Spain.

The tourist office has a list of other bodegas. One of the smaller but worthwhile ones is **Sandeman**, who do a good tour (pre-book).

Costa de la Luz

La Cartuja
Carretera Jerez-Medina Km 9, **T** 956 156 465. *Gardens open Mon-Sat 0930-1115, 1245-1830*. Yeguada de la Cartuja, Carretera Medina Sidonia-El Portal Km 6.5, *T 956 162 809. Sat 1100, €10. Map 6, D4, p257*

Ten kilometres from the city en route to Medina Sidonia, La Cartuja, a beautiful Carthusian monastery, is still occupied by a community of the white-robed monks. It was here that the Cartujano breed of horse was developed and refined (see p74). Visits to the monastery have been suspended pending restoration work, but it's well worth dropping by to admire the harmonious Baroque façade and take a stroll in the gardens. Zurbarán's superb series of paintings for the monastery church can now be seen in the Cádiz museum (see p41).

One of the most important Carthusian horse studs, **Yeguada de la Cartuja**, is located off the road between Medina Sidonia and El Portal, a few kilometres beyond the La Cartuja monastery. There's a weekly tour of the stables including a show and various runnings; it's advisable to reserve this in advance.

White towns of Cádiz

East of Jerez, and stretching into Málaga province, the famous 'white towns' of Andalucía preserve much of their original Moorish street plan and are spectacular, whether viewed from afar, atop their steep hills, or from up close, lost in their webs of narrow streets. Arcos de la Frontera and Medina Sidonia are far from being quaint little villages; they were important Moorish and Christian cities, the homes of dukes and nobles who have left them with a stunning architectural legacy of palaces and churches. Arcos is the more visited and has an impressive collection of characterful accommodation.

▸▸ *See Sleeping p108, Eating and drinking p136, Bars and clubs p154*

Arcos de la Frontera
There are half-hourly buses to and from Jerez (€2, 45 mins) on weekdays, and a few daily at weekends. There are 6 daily buses to Cádiz (3 at weekends, €4.30, 1 hr 15 mins), and 4 to Ronda (2 hrs), as well as a couple to Sevilla. Buses leave from the station on Los Alcaldes near the main road to Jerez at the bottom of town. There are half-hourly buses from here up into the old town. Map 6, D5, p257

One of the most striking of the white towns, and the most westerly of the series that runs into Málaga province, old Arcos has a dramatic position on a hilltop, with many buildings worriedly peering over the edge of the crumbly cliffs. Approaching from Jerez, you won't get this viewpoint; it's worth taking the Avenida Duque de Arcos that runs along the bottom of the cliff for the best view. Arcos has an ancient history, having been founded by the Romans as Arco Briga; it was expanded by the Moors and even became the seat of its own little *taifa* kingdom. It held out against the Reconquest until 1264; it can't have been the easiest spot on earth to conquer.

While the new town sprawls unattractively from the main road, the older part is a perfectly preserved network of narrow streets, with a North African feeling of white buildings studded with the sandstone façades of *palacios* and churches. From the new town, the main street, Calle Corredera, climbs along the ridge of the hill up to the heart of the *casco antiguo*, the Plaza del Cabildo, which has a mirador with fine views.

Opposite stands the **Basílica de Santa María** (*Mon-Fri 1000-1300, 1530-1830, Sat 1000-1400, €1.50, closed Jan and Feb*), whose buttresses you had to pass under while ascending the street. The Baroque belfry looks a bit curious tacked on to what is essentially a late Gothic church. It's surprisingly small inside, but you can admire the high panelled golden *retablo* topped by Plateresque stonework. It seems a pity that for some reason the congregation face the other way these days. The sacristy has a fine frieze and ceiling; but it's the exterior west façade that is the real masterpiece, an Isabelline Gothic work with very ornate piers decorated with niches and pinnacles.

On the west side of the Plaza del Cabildo, the castle looms. While it was once the Moorish stronghold, it owes its current appearance to the 15th century. It's unfortunately a private residence and not open to the public.

From here, wander to your heart's content through the narrow streets to the east. There are several palacios, with delicately carved façades, and another interesting church, **San Pedro** (*Mon-Sat 1000-1300, 1600-1900, Sun 1000-1330, €1*), which has a fine Baroque belltower and another excellent painted *retablo*.

Following a lane around the back of San Pedro, the street leads downhill to another fine mirador with 270° views over the fertile *vega* below town and the artificial lake that gives citizens relief from the summer heat.

Medina Sidonia

Tourist information office, opposite the church. *Daily 1000-
1400, 1600-1800 (on Sat mornings it transfers itself to a kiosk on
Plaza España). There are 6-7 buses daily from Cádiz to Medina
Sidonia, and hourly buses from Jerez. Map 6, F5, p257*

This ancient white town was originally settled by the
Phoenicians. The Romans fortified the hilltop and called the
colony Asido Caesarina; it later became an important Visigothic
and Moorish town. It was recaptured under Guzmán El Bueno,
the hero of the defence of Tarifa; the town and lands were
granted to him and he thus became the first duke of Medina
Sidonia. This aristocratic line has traditionally been Spain's most
powerful and, for centuries, the dukes were the country's largest
private landowners. Medina Sidonia is less touristy than most of
the white towns and only 35 km from Jerez.

The town has preserved a rich array of remnants from its
various ruling civilizations. Dominating the small walled precinct
at the top of the hill is the church of **Santa María la Mayor la
Coronada** (*daily 1030-1400, 1600-1830, €1*). It preserves the
courtyard of the original mosque; the mossy belltower was once
its minaret. The staggering *retablo* dominates the Gothic interior,
a memorable 16th-century work with five rows of panels
depicting the life of Christ painted and sculpted by Juan Bautista
Vásquez and Melchor Turín. There's also a fine sculpted Christ by
Pedro Roldán.

Plaza España, the main square, is a long elegant space with
several terraced cafés and the Ayuntamiento at one end.

Other things to look out for while wandering around town
are the restored 10th-century horseshoe entrance gate, the
Arco de la Pastora, and lofty vaulted Roman sewers. The castle
is poorly preserved.

South from Cádiz

The most enticing stretch of the Costa de la Luz runs south from Cádiz to Gibraltar. It has a range of vast sandy Atlantic beaches, some calm, some with serious surf, and is happily free of much of the overdevelopment that plagues the Mediterranean coasts. Backing the beaches are rolling pastures which rise to a chain of green hills. There's a variety of settlements to choose from, from the new-age vibe of Los Caños de Meca to the Moorish ambience of Vejer via the windsurfers' haven of Tarifa. What attracts the sailboarders, however, is the wind, which is more or less a constant presence, from the easterly poniente to the howling westerly levante, which "wails through the streets like a thousand crying children". Don't despair; where else can you exfoliate and suntan at the same time? There's plenty to do away from the sand; the Roman ruins at Baelo Claudia are impressive, the castle at Tarifa was venue for one of the Reconquista's most famous acts of courage, and the alleys of Vejer are a delight to wander.

One of the most exciting aspects of this coast is that you can see the mountains of Morocco looming to the south across the Straits. It's quite feasible to pop across for a day-trip or longer, as Tanger is just 35 minutes on the boat from Tarifa, or 70 minutes on a ferry from the port of Algeciras.

▸▸ *See Sleeping p110, Eating and drinking p137*

Chiclana de la Frontera and around
Map 6, F4, p257

Heading south from Cádiz, the first stretch of coast has been more or less ruined by *urbanizaciones* and resort development. The former is

! Probably the greatest of all flamenco artists, the gaunt genius Camarón de la Isla (1950-92), was born in San Fernando, just south of Cádiz.

largely due to the fact that Cádiz itself, on a narrow promontory, has nowhere to expand, so the towns to the south are becoming satellite suburbs. The town of Chiclana is one of the largest of these, and not an especially tempting place. It's a little inland, on the edge of the *marismas* (marshes); on the coast is the fishing village of **Sancti Petri**, whose small islet has the remains of a Phoenician temple and a medieval castle. The atmosphere of the area has been severely compromised by the building of nearby **Novo Sancti Petri**, a sprawling and tasteless resort.

Conil de la Frontera and El Palmar

Tourist office, **T** 956 440 501, near the Comes bus stop on Calle Carretera, Conil. *There are 12 Comes buses from Cádiz to Conil on weekdays, falling to 6 at weekends, and 4 from Jerez. Map 6, F4, p257*

Likeable Conil is the first place south of Cádiz really worth a stop. A sizeable fishing town with an excellent long beach, it becomes a busy but pleasant resort in summer. The **Torre de Guzmán** near the beach is the town's main monument; it is all that is left of a castle once built by Guzmán El Bueno.

Directly in front of the Paseo Marítimo is the beach of **Los Bateles**, usually particularly good for families with children as it's calm and shallow. It stretches south to El Palmar – a popular surfing spot, see below – and north to **La Fontanilla** beach, with plenty of clifftop development but a couple of fine summer *chiringuitos* and a popular seafood restaurant. North of here, the cliffs follow the curve of the bay round to the fishing port and lighthouse. Just before the port is a turning to **Cala El Aceite**, a secluded and popular cove of perfect sand. Behind the port, the tree-shaded river is a pleasant spot for less blustery swimming and picnics.

The quiet little hamlet of El Palmar, a few kilometres south of Conil de la Frontera, makes a very appealing place to relax. The beach, a continuation of Conil's, is fantastic.

★ Sandy beaches

Best

- Playa de Mazagón, at its best a few kilometres east of Mazagón itself, p53
- El Palmar, just south of Conil de la Frontera, p82
- Los Caños de Meca, p83
- Zahara de los Atunes, p87
- Playa de los Lances, Tarifa, p90

Los Caños de Meca and Cabo Trafalgar

Buses run along the coast between Conil and Barbate a couple of times a day; on Mon-Fri there are also 2 buses to and from Cádiz. Map 6, G4, p257

A short way further south from El Palmar, the villages of **Zahora** and Los Caños de Meca more or less blend into each other. Between them is a beautiful sandy cape with a lighthouse, Cabo Trafalgar (stress on the last syllable around here). If you've ever fed the pigeons or waited for a night-bus under Nelson's column in London, it's because of what happened just off here on 21 October, 1805. A combined French and Spanish fleet were pulverized by a smaller but technically superior British force; Spanish naval power never really recovered from this devastating defeat. The victorious British commander Horatio Nelson was killed early in the engagement; his Spanish counterpart Admiral Gravina also perished, as did over 15,000 men (90% of them Spanish and French) and 18 ships.

Los Caños de Meca is one of the finest beaches on this coast and is named for the cascades of water that pour from its low cliffs. Unfortunately, the water from these springs (*caños*) is not as clean as it used to be. The village was once home to a hippy community, and there's still a relaxed alternative atmosphere to the place even in the height of summer, with beach parties and plenty of people sleeping rough under the stars.

Barbate

There are hourly buses from Cádiz to Barbate; buses run from here along the coast to Conil via Los Caños de Meca. Map 6, G5, p257

The road from Los Caños to Barbate climbs through sand dunes covered with umbrella pines; this zone, known as **La Breña**, is encompassed in a parque natural. Walking in the peaceful woods makes a relaxing break from life on the beach.

The road then descends to Barbate, passing a spectacular sandy beach before winding its way past the new marina. Barbate itself is a fishing town; even its staunchest fans (of whom there are many) wouldn't describe it as a beautiful place, but it's a very enjoyable, friendly, earthy sort of place; this is the 'real Spain' in a way that many of the resorts of the Costa del Sol further east will never be again.

Barbate makes its living from tuna, and the elaborate, traditional fixed nets known as *almadrabas* have changed little since Roman times. The town is famous for its *salazones* (salt-cured fish preserves) and there's a shop-museum on the outskirts of the town where you can try and buy these tasty products (see Shopping, p176).

Barbate is full of good places to eat; just stroll along the beachside **Paseo Marítimo** and take your pick. As well as the catch of the day, it has a strong reputation for *churrasco*, grilled pork ribs in a hot sauce. As one local fisherman said: "You can't fight the tuna if you only eat fish!". Also worth a visit is the small **Mercado de Abastos**, a very traditional food market. Old Spanish customs continue here; while the men are out fishing in the morning, the women go to the market, buy fresh food, and cook up a massive lunch for when hubby gets home.

Between the beach and the main road through town is the old part of town; seek out **Calle Real**, a picturesque old street that was once the heart of the community. Barbate is also one of the few towns in Spain where you can still see the street names from the Franco era; the main drag is called Avenida Generalísimo. This

The coast of death

Recent surveys have suggested that some 70% of Moroccans would live in the EU if they were allowed to. This is a remarkable statistic and one that is reflected in the large numbers of Africans that attempt to enter Spain illegally by crossing the Straits of Gibraltar in boats. While Spaniards regularly rate this as one of their major life concerns (which would be laughable did it not indicate how seriously media hysteria has wormed its way into the modern psyche), by far the most serious issue is not how many make it, but the alarming numbers who don't. Often paying an entire life's savings to make the journey – or more, as unscrupulous brokers often take a huge cut of any future earnings – these souls embark in unseaworthy vessels (known as *pateras*) into one of the narrowest, but most treacherous, stretches of water on the planet. In the last few years, thousands of bodies have been found washed up on beaches in Cádiz province. The Spanish government has been primarily concerned with preventing landings rather than saving lives at sea – after all, these 'illegals' might have the nerve to try again if they are rescued. Increasing pressure from lobby groups has stepped up coastal patrols and it can only be hoped that these sobering statistics can be reduced, as the issue is already a full-scale human crisis and has revealed a deeply sinister streak in the Spanish government.

isn't really an indication of local politics; Franco used to spend his summer holidays here – the town is still sometimes referred to as Barbate de Franco, and is a little unwilling to ditch the last reminders of those days in the limelight.

Vejer de la Frontera

There are 9 buses to Vejer itself from Cádiz on weekdays and 5 at weekends (€3.50, 50 mins), and very frequent buses to Barbate. For Tarifa or Jerez, you'll need to descend to La Barca de Vejer, on the N340 below town.   Map 6, G4, p257

This white town is situated slightly inland and is one of the gems of this well-endowed province. Set on a high saddle-shaped hill, it's a stunning sight as you approach. The old town, on one of the two brows, is still encircled by its 15th-century walls, which are in an excellent state of preservation and maintain gateways from the original Moorish ramparts. Vejer dates back to Roman times, but still has much of its Moorish feel, with narrow streets and glimpses of patios. Indeed, until relatively recently, many Vejer women wore a *cobija*, a dark cloak covering the whole face but the eyes. Many scholars feel that the decisive battle between the invading Moorish forces and the Visigoths under King Roderic took place near Vejer in 711.

Just by the tourist office is the parish church, **Iglesia del Divino Salvador** (unusual indeed to find a Christian church in Andalucía that is dedicated to Christ rather than his mother). Originally built in the 14th century over the town mosque, it is in Gothic-*mudéjar* style; later additions in the 17th century used a sort of neo-Gothic style to stay faithful to the original design. Around the side of the church are part of the dogtoothed town walls and a gateway.

Beyond here is the **castle**, built by the Moors in the 9th and 10th centuries, but transformed into a 19th-century house. It preserves a horseshoe-arched portal inside the wooden door, but is currently closed to the public. Further along, you come to the Jewish quarter, where there are some gateways in the wall with fine views across to the new town. A local tale relates how a young couple, architects, were cemented up alive in a section of the wall here for painting their house black. At the bottom of the old town is **Plaza de España**, a pretty space with a colourful tiled fountain.

The new part of town has been fairly sensitively designed and doesn't clash at all with the old town. There's little to see apart from a couple of fine whitewashed windmills, which are in the process of being restored to their former glories.

On the N340 south of Vejer is the **Fundación NMAC** (Ctra N340 Km 42.5, **T** 956 455 134, *daily 1000-1400, 1600-1830, 1700-2030 summer*), a contemporary art foundation which stages open-air exhibitions in a large wooded park. Some of the pieces are permanent, some temporary, but there are some extraordinary works usually present, and it's well worth visiting.

Zahara de los Atunes
There are 3-4 daily buses from Cádiz to Zahara run by Comes.
Map 6, G5, p257

This somewhat isolated town has a wild and fantastic sandy beach with big breakers. Its name means 'blossom of the tuna fish', and it is indeed by these large beasts that the town has lived for centuries. The methods of catching the tuna have changed little over the years. Shoals pass along the coast between April and June on their way to spawn in the Mediterranean, returning in July and August. The tuna, which can weigh up to 800 kg, are herded into nets where they are hooked and hauled into the boats. Much of the tuna goes to Japanese and Korean factory ships waiting off shore, but the catch has dwindled in recent years, likely due to overfishing.

The centre of town is likeably ordinary, although some resort development has gone up a couple of kilometres to the south, a district someone was probably paid a lot to name **Atlanterra**.

! Cervantes famously commented in *La Ilustre Fregona* that nobody was truly a rogue unless they had fished tuna for two seasons at Zahara.

▶ Garum

A great variety of fish-based sauces was used for cooking and condiments all over the Roman world, but the most prized was garum, and many ancient writers considered that the finest garum came from the Andalucían coasts. There are still factories in Almuñécar and Baelo Claudia, where this sauce was made.

Garum probably originated with the Greeks, whose basic fish sauce was named *garos*, but the Roman gourmets refined it to the point where Martial stated that the finest was made only from fresh mackerel. Pliny comments that the sauce was made by putting whole fish, fish intestines, and salt together and fermenting the mixture in the sun, before straining off the oozing liquid. Although a variety of spices seem to have been added to the recipe as well, the smell produced during the process was so great that citizens were forbidden to make garum at home. Before wrinkling your nose in disgust, consider what Worcestershire sauce or Gentleman's Relish is...

The finished product was strong-tasting but apparently not stinky; Pliny described it as having the colour of aged honey wine and said that it was sometimes mixed with wine. In cooking, it seems to have been used to give flavour not unlike how salt or southeast Asian fish sauces are employed.

Apart from the superb beach there's nothing much to see but the **Almadraba**, the ruins of the huge tuna *lonja* (market) that stands by the shore. Very quiet outside of summer, there are always a few places open to try the many varieties of tuna, prepared in numerous different styles.

Six kilometres south of Zahara, along the coast road beyond ugly Atlanterra, is **Playa de los Alemanes**. This pretty strip of sand is more sheltered than the Zahara beach, and is backed by wealthy villas.

Bolonia

In summer, buses run to Bolonia from Tarifa, but otherwise it's a 7-km walk from the main road or 1 hr's walk around the coast from Zahara de los Atunes. Map 6, G5, p257

The small village of Bolonia, on a side road populated by red long-horned cattle, is one of the coast's more alternative places, with plenty of new age and hippy travellers giving it a great summer atmosphere. The beach is typical for these parts; that means beautiful, windswept and with clean sand. Although very quiet off season, there are a number of places to stay and eat in summer, as well as the interesting Roman ruins of Baelo Claudia.

Apart from the Roman ruins, the pleasure of Bolonia is simply lingering on the beach. Walking southwards you come to a small point marked by a stone circle that's a fine place to relax by the sea.

Baelo Claudia

Tue-Sat 1000-2000 (spring 1900, winter 1800), Sun 1000-1400, free for EU citizens, €1.50 for others. Map 6, G5, p257

Started as a settlement in the late second century BC, Baelo Claudia rapidly became an important Roman town for its proximity to North Africa and, later, for its production of garum, the fish sauce that was much prized in Rome (see box, p88). The town's street plan is well preserved. The forum has remains of several temples around it, while a theatre, several shops and a market are also identifiable. The inescapable Roman baths are also present. Closer to the sea is the area where the garum was presumably manufactured. The urban area was walled; some traces remain of this. The whole site has a lovely situation overlooking the beach and the bay; hopefully the construction of a luxury hotel by its side won't affect it too much.

Tarifa and around

One of the most relaxed of Andalucían locations, Tarifa is also one of the world's prime destinations for windsurfers and kitesurfers due to the almost constant winds that blow across its excellent sandy beach. A pretty town with a distinct Moorish character, Tarifa is sure to please, not least for the fact that you can nip across to Morocco for lunch on the fast ferry. Summertime isn't the best period to visit, as the small town becomes overcongested, and it's difficult to find accommodation.

▸▸ *See Sleeping p115, Eating and drinking p142, Bars and clubs p155*

---

*Comes buses serve Tarifa, and leave from Av Batalla del Salado near the Puerta de Jerez, **T** 956 657 555. There are 7 daily buses to Cádiz, 3 to Jerez and 4 to Sevilla. In an easterly direction, there are 10 buses to Algeciras (30 mins), falling to 7 on Sun, and 7 to La Línea, the entry point for Gibraltar. 1 bus on weekdays travels to Zahara de los Atunes, Barbate, Los Caños de Meca and Conil. There are 2 buses to Málaga. In summer, there are buses on Sat and Sun to Bolonia.*

*In summer, a local bus company, Bus Tarifa, **T** 647 911 691, runs a service from town up along Playa de los Lances, stopping at the hotels en route, and sometimes going as far as Bolonia. The schedule changes each year, so ring or ask at the tourist office for details.*

From nearby Algeciras, opposite the ferry terminal, Alsina Graells and Portillo run 4 daily services to Granada (3 hrs 50 mins, €17.37), 8 buses direct to Málaga (1 hr 50 mins, €9.33), as well as a similar number via Marbella and the other coastal towns. There are 2 buses to Córdoba (€19.49) and 2 to Jaén (€23.24). From the ferry port itself, Alsa runs long-distance buses to Murcia, Valencia, and Barcelona as well as further-flung destinations in Europe.

! According to one theory, the English word 'tariff' comes from the taxes levied by swashbucklers off the coast of Tarifa to guarantee the safe passage of boats.

> ### Guzmán 'El Bueno'
>
> Tarifa's hero, Guzmán 'El Bueno', was a knight from León who defended the castle against Moorish attackers. The invaders captured his son and threatened to kill him if Guzmán wouldn't yield. The knight allegedly threw down his own dagger to them, saying "I would rather have my honour and no son than my son and no honour". The boy was killed, the city held on, and Guzmán became the first duke of Medina Sidonia for his pains.

Sights

Castillo de Guzmán El Bueno

Calle Guzmán El Bueno s/n, **T** 956 680 993. *Daily 1100-1400, 1600-1800, €1.80, buy your tickets in the stationery shop opposite the entrance. Map 5, F4, p256*

Tarifa's Castillo de Guzmán El Bueno was built in the 10th century by the Moors, partly because of significant piratic activity in the Straits of Gibraltar. After the town was reconquered by Sancho IV (who sits petting a lion in sculptured majesty outside the entrance), the citadel was commanded by Guzmán El Bueno and is named after him. Much of the Moorish structure remains, a bit derelict but basically sturdy; there's a foundation tablet in Arabic over one of the entrances. The keep's interior is a little bare, but used for summer concerts; there's a display on the life of Guzmán here, including various newspaper cartoons parodying his famous action. A second castle sits out on a promontory opposite and is used by the Guardia Civil.

The town's **Ayuntamiento**, as well as the church of **Santa María**, stand on a pretty gardened square near the castle; a fine spot to relax on a sunny day.

San Mateo
Map 5, D5, p256

The main church in town is San Mateo, whose huge blocky
Baroque façade is hard to miss. The interior is more elegant
in 15th-century Gothic, brightened by stained-glass windows.
The sculpture of the saint himself is an exquisitely rendered piece
by Martínez Montañés, several of whose works adorn Sevilla's
cathedral. In a side aisle is an interesting Visigothic tombstone.

Puerta de Jerez
Map 5, C3, p256

At the top of the old town, the well-restored Puerta de Jerez lets
you into or out of central Tarifa through its horseshoe arches.
Once outside, it's worth following around to your right and turning
down **Calle Calzadilla**, where you can admire the best-preserved
section of Tarifa's imposing walls.

If you fancy a light stroll, Tarifa is the start of the GR7
footpath that leads to... Athens. If Greece seems like a bit of a
hike, you can do a shorter section; the path leads through the
pretty natural park of **Los Alcornocales** to hill villages such
as Jimena de la Frontera and beyond.

● *There's not a huge amount to see in Tarifa, but you can't
complain when you've got a 10-km sandy beach with views of Africa
thrown in for free. One of the best viewing spots is the small mirador
and garden on* **Plazuela del Viento***, a couple of blocks east of the
castle. Another fine, if rubbish-strewn viewpoint is the* **Mirador del
Estrecho***, a few kilometres east of Tarifa on the main road.*

! Nelson wanted to be buried in England and not at sea so,
● after his death at Trafalgar the ship's doctor had to place his
body in a barrel of brandy to preserve it while the Victory
was repaired at Gibraltar.

A curious and worrying phenomenon is the extremely high number of suicides in the Tarifa area. While the location would seem ideal for escaping from the worries and tensions of everyday life, there must be more complex factors involved. Psychologists have suggested that the almost constant winds might have some undocumented effect on the psyche. The same winds, however, are being usefully employed (apart from filling windsurfers' sails that is) in the giant windfarms that line the hilltops above the town. While not especially beautiful, it is bewildering to see how many complaints from ecologists they have drawn; as a year-round renewable source of energy, they are surely a significant step in the right direction for a power-hungry society.

Listings

◉ Museums

- **Casa de Martín Alonso Pinzón**, Palos de la Frontera. Set in the house of Columbus' right-hand man, details of their first voyage and of the first Atlantic crossing by plane, p65.
- **Casa Museo Zenobia y Juan Ramón**, Moguer. Typical Andalucían house where the poet Juan Ramón Jiménez lived with his wife, p67.
- **Casa Natal**, Moguer. Childhood home of poet Juan Ramón Jiménez, restored to what it looked like in the late 19th century, p67.
- **Fundación Rafael Alberti**, El Puerto de Santa María. Documents and objects housed in the poet's childhood home, p46.
- **Museo de Cádiz**, Cádiz. Phoenician archaeology, sculptures and monastic paintings, among others, p41.
- **Museo de la Catedral**, Cádiz. Charming building and patio housing various art works and excavated section of Roman road, p36.
- **Museo de la Miel y las Abejas**, Jerez de la Frontera. Watch the bees going about their business and learn about honey-making, p196.
- **Museo de las Cortes**, Cádiz. A huge late 18th-century model of Cádiz and impressive wallpainting of events in 1812, p43.
- **Museo del Mar**, Sanlúcar de Barrameda. Seashells and beachcombing finds, p49.
- **Museo del Mundo Marino**, Matalascañas. Display of dune and maritime ecology focusing on Bahía de Cádiz area, p197.
- **Museo Litográfico Andaluz**, Bóvedas de San Roque s/n, Cádiz T 956 282 663, Tue-Fri 0900-1300, 1600-1900, Sat/Sun 0900-1300. Explores the history of Cádiz's important printmaking industry. **Museo Marín**, Calle Arroyuelo 16, Chiclana de la Frontera, T 956 400 067, Mon-Fri 0900-1300, Sat 0930-1330. A large collection of flamenco dolls.
- **Museo Municipal**, El Puerto de Santa María. Collection of archaeological finds and paintings by local *portuense* artists, p46.
- **Museo Taurino**, Calle Pozo del Olivar 6, Jerez de la Frontera, T 956 323 000, Mon-Sat 1000-1400. Collection of bullfighting memorabilia.

The standard of accommodation in this part of Andalucía is very high; even the most modest of *pensiones* is usually very clean and respectable. Places to stay (*alojamientos*) are divided into two main government-devised categories: *hoteles* (marked H or HR) are graded from one to five stars and occupy their own building, which distinguishes them from many *hostales* (Hs or HsR), which go from one to three stars. Within the latter category, the *pensión* is the standard budget option, typically family-run and occupying a floor of an apartment building. Spanish traditions of hospitality are alive and well; even the simplest of *pensiones* will generally provide a towel and soap, and check-out time is almost uniformly a very civilized midday.

All registered accommodations charge a 7% value added tax; this is often included in the price at cheaper places and may be waived if you pay cash (tut tut). Breakfast isn't usually included. Prices are much cheaper in winter. Also, check the websites of larger hotels for weekend deals; you can save up to 50% on the midweek prices.

Sleeping codes

Price

LL	€150 and over	**C**	€45-59
L	€120-149	**D**	€38-44
AL	€100-119	**E**	€30-37
A	€80-99	**F**	€20-29
B	€60-79	**G**	€19 and under

Prices codes refer to a standard double or twin room, inclusive of the 7% VAT. The rates are generally for high season (June-August on the coast). Occasionally, an area or town will have a short period when prices are hugely exaggerated; this normally corresponds to a festival such as the Cádiz Carnaval. Low-season prices can be significantly lower; up to half in many towns along this coast.

Cádiz

The most characterful sleeping options are the *pensiones* of the old town, but the quality varies significantly. Make sure you see the room first, and keep an eye out for *camas* (beds) signs in windows; these rooms can be a real bargain. You need to book anything for Carnaval several months in advance, and prices for even the most basic rooms are sky-high at this time.

L-A Hotel Playa Victoria, Plaza Ingeniero La Cierva 4,
T 956 205 100, www.palafoxhoteles.com. *Map 1, F12, p251 (off map)* This vast, modern hotel has an unbeatable situation dominating the beach in the new town. Despite its size, it has a reputation for friendly service, and every one of its stylishly furnished doubles has a balcony looking straight over the water. The breakfast buffet is impressive at €9.60, and as long as there's availablity, rooms are significantly cheaper at weekends than during the week.

AL Parador Atlántico, Avenida Duque de Nájera 9, **T** 956 226 905, www.parador.es. *Map 1, D1, p250* Not the nicest of the *paradores*, with a slight feeling of sterility and little character, but with an excellent location at the tip of the Cádiz promontory. Many of the rooms have sea views, and there's an outdoor pool looking over the Atlantic. Some of the rooms are fitted out with old furniture and have much more style to them.

A Hospedería Las Cortes de Cádiz, Calle San Francisco 9, **T** 956 212 668, www.hotellascortes.com. *Map 1, B7, p251* This newly opened spot is right in the heart of the old town and makes a great base. Built around a central patio, it's all yellow ochre and white balcony rails, giving a cool, light feel. The rooms are inviting, with high wooden bedheads and modern conveniences such as digital TV and air-conditioning. Pick an exterior room if you can; the noise from the bustling street is worth it for the extra light. There are views from the roof as well as a gymnasium and sauna.

B Hotel Francia y París, Plaza San Francisco 2, **T** 956 212 318, **F** 956 222 348. *Map 1, B6, p250* With an enviable location on a pretty square close to the Museo de Cádiz, this elegant hotel is set around a central patio. Some of the top-floor rooms have views across the bay, and all are very comfortable and well equipped for the price. Limited parking available. One thing to bear in mind is that the square is a riot of cheerful outdoor drinking from midnight onwards on Thursday to Saturday nights, so make sure you don't have a room overlooking it.

B Hotel Regio, Avenida Ana de Viya 11, **T** 956 279 331, www.hotelregiocadiz.com. *Map 1, E12, p251 (off map)* One of the best options in the beach zone, this modern and functional hotel has well-equipped rooms and competent staff. Rooms on the front side can be noisy but also have the bustle of life on the main road to observe.

C Hostal Bahía, Calle Plocia 5, **T** 956 259 061, hostalbahia@terra.es. *Map 1, D10, p251* Right in the heart of things near Plaza San Juan de Dios, this small *hostal* is one of the best options in the old town. All rooms have a/c, TV, balcony and modern bathroom, and the management are helpful. The rooms are a touch spartan for the price; try haggling for discount, although in the end it's worth it for the location.

D Hostal Centro Sol, Calle Manzanares 7, **T** 956 283 103, centralsol@wanadoo.es. *Map 1, C8, p251* Small and welcoming modernized *hostal* with a café attached. Rooms, arranged around a pleasant patio, have spotless but tiny bathrooms and cable TV and are comfortable, if a tad overpriced.

E Hostal Fantoni, Calle Flamenco 5, **T** 956 282 704. *Map 1, D9, p251* A very attractive place near the tourist office. Built around a tile-decked patio, it's a sparklingly clean place. The rooms can be a little dark, but are still modern and offer plenty of value. There are more expensive and comfortable rooms with en suite available (**C-D**).

F Cuatro Naciones, Calle Plocia 3, **T** 956 255 539. *Map 1, D10, p251* Simple but clean rooms with tartan blankets In a very central location. There's a modern shared bathroom, the place is surprisingly quiet, and the management tolerant and friendly. Under different managements and locations, Cuatro Naciones has been a *fonda* for well over a century and a half.

F Hostal Colón, Calle Marqués de Cádiz 6, **T** 956 285 351. *Near the town hall. Map 1, D9, p251* The best of the cheap options on this street. Clean and proper rooms with or without bath; some with balconies overlooking the street.

G Quo Qadis, Calle Diego Arias 1, **T** 956 221 939, quoqadis@infocadiz.com. *Near the Teatro Falla. Map 1, D3, p250*

This large independent hostel makes an excellent base. There's a big roof terrace and clean dorm rooms for €7-12 per person depending on the season. There are meals available too, and plenty of information on the city. There are also good rooms on offer here (**E**). There's a 0300 curfew, but the Cádiz nightlife can easily keep you going until it opens again in the morning. Breakfast included, and small discount for those on bikes.

El Puerto de Santa María

As well as being an intriguing place in its own right, its excellent transport connections mean that El Puerto makes a good base for the Carnaval at Cádiz. While it's easier to bag a room here than in Cádiz itself, you'll still need to book well in advance.

LL Hotel Monasterio San Miguel, Calle Larga 27, **T** 956 540 440, www.jale.com. *Map 2, A4, p252 (off map)* One of the more luxurious spots around and a place where the king himself has laid his head, this former monastery is now a large and comfortable hotel with a rainforest garden, swimming pool, top restaurant and antique furniture. Rooms are large, with particularly comfortable beds. Summer prices hover around the €170 mark for a standard double; this rate includes breakfast.

AL Casa de los Leones, Calle La Placilla 2, **T** 956 875 277. *Next to the food market. Map 2, C2, p252* A beautifully renovated 18th-century house which holds exhibitions and is named after the creatures on the pillars either side of the front door. The house is centred around a patio; the galleries are exquisite, with chessboard tiling, wooden ceilings and wrought-iron balustrades. The accommodation is in spacious apartments with dining table, kitchen, microwave, fridge and washing machine; they are available with one or two double bedrooms and are remarkably cheap (**C**) off season. Recommended.

AL Hotel Los Cántaros, Calle Curva 6, **T** 956 540 240, www.hotelloscantaros.com. *Just behind the seafood strip. Map 2, C5, p252* This attractive and hospitable hotel has bright and cheery rooms decorated in differing colours and styles. Once a prison, it couldn't have changed more. Prices drop significantly off season (**B**). Parking available.

D Hostal Sherry, Calle Veneroni 1, **T** 956 870 902. *Between the castle and the riverfront. Map 2, F6, p252* A relaxed and friendly spot in a charming if faded old building. The rooms are clean and come with fan and bathroom.

E Pensión Manolo, Calle Jesús de los Milagros 18, **T** 956 857 525. *Map 2, D5, p252* A fine budget choice, set right in the heart of things. The place is centred around a pretty patio; the rooms are small but clean and adequate; some have balcony. The **Esperanza**, opposite (**T** 956 873 593), is similarly priced, more modern, but slightly less charming.

Camping
Camping Playa Las Dunas, Paseo Marítimo La Puntilla, **T** 956 872 210. *By the beach. Map 2, H6, p252 (off map)* A large site with excellent facilities including a swimming pool, and party atmosphere in summer.

Sanlúcar de Barrameda

There are few accommodation options in Sanlúcar, and it can be tough to find a room on-spec in summer.

A Hotel Tartaneros, Calle Tartaneros 8, **T** 956 362 044, **F** 956 360 045. *Map 3, F3, p253* A beautiful early 20th-century building at the head of the avenue just near Plaza del Cabildo. The decor is rather staid, but the rooms are comfortable enough and have facilities such as minibar, safe and satellite TV. There's also a large attractive patio to have a drink or breakfast.

A Posada de Palacio, Calle Caballeros 11, **T/F** 956 365 060, www.posadadepalacio.com. *Opposite the Palacio de Orléans-Borbon. Map 3, H4, p253* A lovely spot set in a smart 18th-century *palacio*. The house has a lovely patio, sunny terrace, and swimming pool; the rooms (of which there's a variety) are furnished in understated belle epoque style, with charming beds, plush armchairs and balconies overlooking the garden. Recommended.

C Hotel Los Helechos, Plaza Madre de Dios 9, **T** 956 361 349, www.hotelloshelechos.com. *Town centre. Map 3, G3, p253* This hotel is built around two pleasant patios. The rooms are modern and comfortable, offering fairly good value for money, particularly off season (**D**).

E Pensión La Bohemia, Calle Don Claudio 1, **T** 956 369 599. *Near the Iglesia de Santo Domingo. Map 3, F6, p253* Lovely budget accommodation. The place absolutely gleams, so thoroughly are its pretty *azulejos* scrubbed; the rooms are cosy and have good if small modern bathrooms attached. Recommended.

F Hostal Blanca Paloma, Plaza de San Roque 9, **T** 956 363 644. *Map 3, G4, p253* Handy central *pensión* looking over this busy square. Rooms are basic but comfortable, equipped with fan and washbasin; the shared bathrooms are clean. Good value even in summer.

Chipiona

D Pensión Andalucía, Calle Larga 14, **T** 956 370 705. *Near the lighthouse. Map 6, D3, p257* Has a friendly owner and good clean rooms which are much cheaper outside of the summer season.

Coto Doñana

Mazagón

AL Parador de Mazagón, Carretera Huelva-Matalascañas Km 30, **T** 959 536 300, www.parador.es. By far the best option, this modern but sensitively designed hotel nestles in the dunes above a top stretch of beach 3 km east of the centre. On the other side, its attractive gardens give way to the pines of the dune-forest. The restaurant is excellent and the rooms cool and well appointed. There's also a tennis court, gym and swimming pool.

B Hotel Albaida, Urbanización El Faro s/n, **T** 959 376 029. *A 10-minute stroll from the centre of town.* A small and likeable hotel. The rooms are a/c and the establishment is close to the sea, but far from being resorty. There's a popular restaurant serving local specialities.

E Hostal Acuario, Avenida Fuentepiña 29, **T** 959 377 286. This is set right on the pedestrian street at the centre of town. It's a simple and friendly place; the rooms are newly refurbished and have bright small bathrooms and cosy beds. Recommended.

E-F Albergue de Mazagón, Calle de la Barca s/n, **T** 959 536 262. An official youth hostel in pine-wooded grounds near the campsites (see below), with four-berth cabins and bathroom.

F Pensión Alvarez Quintero, Calle Hernández de Soto 174, **T** 959 376 169. Despite its rather grand *cortijo*-style entrance, this is a budget option, with basic rooms with bathroom that are quiet, adequate and near the beach. Often closed in winter, so ring ahead. From the centre, head down towards the beach and take the last street on the left before reaching it.

Camping

Camping Doñana Playa, T 959 536 281. *7 km east of Mazagón.*
It seems like an entire town, stretching from the main road right to
the beach where there's a picturesque ruined watchtower. All
facilities and open year round, although it can be very crowded
during the summer days, as non-campers pay a fee to use the
complex as a base for a day at the beach.

Camping La Fontanilla, T 959 536 237, and **Camping Playa
Mazagón**, T 959 376 208. *Near each other at the eastern end of
Mazagón.* Both are by the beach, are comprehensively equipped
and are open year round.

Matalascañas

The main reason to stay in Matalascañas is the summer nightlife;
otherwise El Rocío or Mazagón make happier choices. There are
several pricey beachside complexes 1 km west of town.

B Hostal Tamarindos, Avenida de las Adelfas 31, T 959 430
119. Clean, bright and very much cheaper (**E**) outside of high
summer. It's not far from the tourist office and a 10-second sprint
to the beach.

Camping

Rocío Playa, 1 km west of town, T 959 430 238. A huge campsite
which is a party centre of its own in summer.

El Rocío

A El Cortijo de los Mimbrales, Carretera El
Rocío-Matalascañas s/n, T 959 442 237, F 959 442 443. *4 km
south of El Rocío.* This tasteful complex of casas rurales is the
best place to stay in the area. There are several self-contained

houses, some with one bedroom, some with two and all with charming rustic decoration and fitted kitchen and fireplace. There's a swimming pool, gardens to stroll in and an excellent hearty and generous restaurant. The helpful staff can also arrange activities in the area. Recommended.

B Hotel Toruñoaz, Pla del Acebuchal 22, **T** 959 442 323, hoteltoruno@terra.es. *East of the church.* By far the most enticing of El Rocío's accommodations, this hotel is situated on the edge of the marshes. Excellent service is complemented by thoughtful Spanish-rustic decoration; many rooms have views over the wetlands and all have TV, a/c and minibar. The restaurant is also good. Recommended.

E Pensión Cristina, Calle El Real 32, **T** 959 442 413. *On a plaza near the sanctuary.* This offers clean rooms that are bright and pleasant, with bathroom, but slightly overpriced. The restaurant is good and cheap (except at weekends); the swordfish is definitely worth a punt if it's in the kitchen.

Lugares Colombinos

Palos de la Frontera

There are a couple of accommodation options in Palos, which makes a tranquil enough base.

B Hotel La Pinta, Calle Rábida 79, **T** 959 350 511, **F** 959 530 164. Right in the centre of town on the main street. Large cool rooms, many with balcony, and free parking right opposite; it's the best place to stay in the area. Prices outside of summer are very reasonable (**D**); there's a pleasing feel to the place and it has a warmly decorated restaurant with a *menú* for €9.62.

G Pensión Rábida, Calle Rábida 9, **T** 959 350 163. A simple tapas bar with rooms that are very basic and very cheap. The shared bathroom is clean though, and the bar is a fine local place with a small patio terrace.

Moguer

Moguer, somewhat surprisingly, has no hotels, but there are a couple of good budget hostales.

E Hostal Platero, Calle Sor (Santa) Angela de la Cruz 4, **T** 959 372 159. In a pretty house with green balconies near the Convento de Santa Clara. The rooms are well equipped for the price, with small bathroom and TV and the place is efficiently maintained.

F Pensión Alonso Niño, Calle Alonso Niño 13, around the corner from Hostal Platero. A spot with plenty of character and friendly owners. Built around a sweet patio, the rooms are simple but satisfying, with shower but shared toilet.

Jerez de la Frontera

AL Hotel Bellas Artes, Plaza del Arroyo 45, **T** 956 348 430, www.hotelbellasartes.com. *Opposite the cathedral. Map 4, F4, p254* This fairly recent addition has been a real shot in the arm for the Jerez accommodation scene. An elegant but friendly spot set in a beautiful 18th-century house, its walls are in soothing pastel colours and thoughtfully decorated with paintings, including some imaginative woodcut prints. The rooms are very attractive too; nab one on the street if you can, as they're much lighter. Some have stone vaulting, while others feature old-style bathtubs. The suites aren't great value, but include a jacuzzi. There's a roof terrace looking right at the cathedral. Prices include a good breakfast. Recommended.

A Hotel La Albarizuela, Calle Honsario 6, **T** 956 346 862, **F** 956 346 686. *Map 4, F8, p255* Stylish modern hotel, all clouded glass, stencilled lettering and white minimalism, recalling the chalky *albariza* sherry soil after which the hotel is named. The rooms are very clean and attractive, the bathrooms good, and the staff friendly. Plenty of value off season like most of Jerez's hotels.

B Hotel Trujillo, Calle Medina 36, **T** 956 342 438. *Map 4, G8, p255* One of the city's more charming hotels, this is set in a stately orange townhouse with a rather grand galleried central patio with carved wooden ceilings. The rooms are comfortable and in the process of being modernized. Management is curious but friendly enough, and there's parking available.

C Hotel Nova, Calle Arcos 13, **T** 956 332 138, www.hotelnovacentro.com. *Map 4, F8, p255* This central hotel has just been expanded and refitted, so the rooms are clean and modern, with plenty of light and standard conveniences. A rambling place in a pretty pink building, this is a friendly and convenient base that's very cheap off season.

D-F San Andrés I & II, Calle Morenos 12, **T** 956 340 983, **F** 956 343 196. *Map 4, E7, p255* This is a two-in-one place, a *hostal* and hotel. Both have beautiful patios full of tropical plants and attractive rooms, some with balconies, the hotel's with modern bathroom, and both with heating. Friendly owners and a comfortable atmosphere.

E Hostal Las Palomas, Calle Higueras 17, **T** 956 343 773. *Map 4, G8, p255* Likeable budget option with rooms around a nice light patio on a quiet street. They're good value for money, and are attractively furnished and roomy; some are better than others so ask to see a couple.

E Hostal Sanvi, Calle Morenos 10, **T** 956 345 624. *Not far from Calle Larga.* *Map 4, E7, p255* Run by a friendly family, this is a very likeable option on a quiet street. The rooms are small but colourful and have fine modern bathrooms. They have no exterior windows but open onto the airy central corridor. Parking available for €6 per day. Recommended.

E-F Albergue Juvenil, Avenida Carrero Blanco 30, **T** 956 143 901, **F** 956 143 263. *A 20-minute walk south of the centre, or catch bus No 13 from Plaza del Arenal.* *Map 4, H3, p254 (off map)* A well-equipped hostel with a pool and accommodation in double rooms. Cheaper if you're under 26.

White towns of Cádiz

Arcos de la Frontera

AL Parador Casa del Corregidor, Plaza del Cabildo s/n, **T** 956 700 500, www.parador.es. *Right on the main square.* Fabulous views out from the clifftop, this smart hotel is located in a typical Andalucían mansion, slightly severe from the outside, but with beautiful interior patios. All the rooms are comfortable, but try to grab one with views over the *vega* rather than onto the square.

B Hotel El Convento, Calle Maldonado 2, **T** 956 702 333, hotelconvento@terra.es. A beautifully restored old monastery in the heart of the village, this recommendable option has very hospitable owners. The rooms are elegant and well looked after, with modern bathrooms and a/c; those with a terrace cost somewhat more, but they're all sound value.

B La Casa Grande, Calle Maldonado 10, **T/F** 956 703 930. *In the centre of the old town.* A tiny, individual hotel with only four rooms in a pretty-as-a-picture mansion. There are charming doubles and a couple of suites, all decorated with a personal Andalucían touch; the beds have big fluffy pillows and, to give a tropical touch, mosquito nets. The roof terrace is the highlight, staring right at the church of San Pedro.

E Hostal San Marcos, Calle Marqués de Torresoto 6, **T** 956 700 721. A small and quiet *pensión* with a charming roof terrace and light, clean rooms with a/c and bathroom at a very good price. Recommended.

E-F Pensión Callejón de las Monjas, Calle Deán Espinosa 4, **T** 956 702 302. This small, budget choice is virtually under the buttresses of the Santa María church. The rooms aren't exactly spacious, but they're cheap and central; they come with or without bath and some have a/c. If there's nobody about, ask next door.

Camping
Camping Lago de Arcos, Santiscal s/n, **T** 956 708 333. *By the lake below the town.* A well-equipped campsite, open year-round and with a swimming pool, shop and restaurant.

Medina Sidonia

A Hotel Medina Sidonia, Plaza Llanete de Herederos s/n, **T** 956 794 092, www.tugasa.com. A hotel on a quiet street near the church that is set in a very elegantly converted palacio with an attractive whitewashed patio.

F Hostal Amalia, Plaza de España 6, **T** 956 410 035. A very likeable cheapie on the main square. The doubles have bathroom and some overlook the plaza.

South from Cádiz

Conil de la Frontera and El Palmar

Accommodation becomes pricey in July and August, but is otherwise reasonable.

L Hotel Fuerte Conil, Playa de la Fontanilla s/n, Conil, **T** 956 443 344, www.fuertehoteles.com. Set in beautiful gardens on the beachfront, this large and popular hotel has several classes of room, including some with fantastic views. The prices vary alarmingly according to the season, with August prices significantly higher.

AL Hotel Almadraba, Calle Señores Curas 4, Conil, **T** 956 456 037, www.hotelalmadrabaconil.com. This likeable small central hotel is built around a cool patio. There's a roof terrace with sea views and plenty of rays. The rooms are bright and colourful and furnished with all conveniences, including minibar and internet jack. The price code reflects the height of summer; off-season rooms fall to as little as €60 for a double.

B Hostal La Conileña, Calle Arrumbadores 1, Conil, **T** 956 444 140, www.hostal-laconilena.com. A good place to stay with attractive rooms that have excellent modern facilities including minibar, hydromassage bath and satellite TV. The friendly owners even screen films at night. Prices include breakfast and become very cheap off season (**E**).

D Casa Francisco, El Palmar, **T** 956 232 786. A great place right on the beach with a fine cheap restaurant. It's just the place for a relaxing break by the sea, and honest and comfortable without being frilly. Closed January to mid-March.

Camping
Camping El Palmar, **T** 956 232 161. *Near the village of El Palmar, and 1 km back from the sea.* This is a popular base for surfers.

Los Caños de Meca and Cabo Trafalgar

There are many places to stay, but most are overpriced in summer and closed in winter.

A-D Casas Karen, Calle Fuente del Madroño 6, **T** 956 437 067, karen@jet.es. A delightful complex with a range of accommodation in characterful buildings that include a barn and thatched huts. There are hammocks to lounge about in and a very friendly owner. The apartments all have a kitchen and are available for well-priced weekly rentals. Recommended.

B El Palomar de la Breña, **T** 956 435 003, www.palomardelabrena.com. *Located 6 km from Los Caños de Meca, taking the Barbate road for 3 km, and then left into the umbrella-pine forest for another 3 km.* A very peaceful spot to stay in the middle of the duney *parque natural* with ample grounds for strolling and the largest dovecote in the world! There are eight rooms, stylishly laid out; all have a balcony and view. There's also a restaurant that specializes in chargrilled meats. Prices include breakfast.

C Pensión Mar de Frente, Calle Trafalgar 3, **T** 956 437 025. *At the southern end of town, beyond the Barbate turn-off at the end of the beach road.* Attractive accommodation. Several of the rooms have balconies right over the beach; these are enchanting, although rooms without balcony are significantly cheaper.

D El Volapié, Carretera Faro de Trafalgar s/n, **T** 956 437 091. *At the beginning of the road that leads to the Cabo Trafalgar* *lighthouse*. This colourful bar/restaurant has 10 simple rooms, all of which have great enclosed balconies where you can sit and listen to the Atlantic roar. The rooms are smallish, but have comfortable beds, decent bathrooms, and rustic esparto curtains. Normally open year round.

D **Hostal Los Caños**, 6 km from Los Caños de Meca, **T** 956 437 176. *Above a supermarket in the centre of town.* This hostal has unremarkable but decent rooms with bathroom and TV; it is open year round and is significantly cheaper off season.

Camping
Camping Faro de Trafalgar, Avenida de las Acacias s/n, **T** 956 437 017. This excellent shady campsite is open year round and has a great atmosphere in summer. There are tennis courts, a swimming pool and minigolf on site.

Barbate

A **Hotel El Chili**, Calle Real 1, **T** 956 454 033, www.madreselva hotel.com Situated at the head of Barbate's most appealing street, this hotel is decorated in some style in a manner more commonly associated with rural retreats. The air-conditioned rooms have modern bathrooms and attractive wooden furniture and wrought-iron beds. There's an inviting bar downstairs and a pretty lounge and restaurant. Breakfast is included in the price, although you may be able to negotiate a cheaper rate and go hungry.

C **Hotel Atlántico**, Avenida Generalísimo 15, **T** 956 431 388, www.arrakis.es/~hotelatlantico. In a town of few sleeping options, this is a reliable choice on the main street. The rooms are clean and as they should be; they are cool in summer and slightly chilly in winter. The off-season prices and the

welcome from an engaging old *barbateño* make it well
worthwhile however.

Vejer de la Frontera

B Convento de San Francisco, La Plazuela s/n, **T** 956 451 001,
www.tugasa.com. Stylishly austere rooms with modern
conveniences and antique furniture in a converted
Franciscan monastery.

B La Casa del Califa, Plaza de España 16, **T** 956 447 730,
hotel@vejer.com. A bewitching spot, a warren-like place part
of which was once where farmers paid their wheat tithes to the
local authorities, and part of which was once an Inquisition
dungeon. It's perfectly fitted in the old structure, with
odd-shaped rooms decorated In quiet Moorish style. There's a
variety on offer, but all have white walls, plenty of light,
varnished wooden furniture, TV, phone, heating and a/c.
The pricier ones have stereo, tea-making facilities and comfy
divans. There's a fabulous terrace too. Highly recommended.

E Hostal Buena Vista, Calle Manuel Machado 4, **T** 956 450 969. *In
the new town*. Spick and span rooms with bathroom and television
in the new town; some have fine views of the village.

Zahara de los Atunes

A Hotel Gran Sol, Calle Sánchez Rodríguez s/n, **T** 956 439 309,
www.hotelgransol.com. Right on the beach, with burnished
copper domes, has all the comfort you would expect from this
level of Spanish hotel and has an attractive annexe with
swimming pool.

C **Hostal Marina**, Calle Manuel Mora s/n, **T** 956 439 009.
Although overpriced in high summer, this is a very good deal
for the rest of the year (**E**). Run out of the Hotel Doña Lola at
the entrance to the town, it has excellent rooms with bathroom
which make a fine base for a beach stay.

D **Hostal Nicolás**, Calle María Luisa 13, **T** 956 439 274.
A welcoming option on the main street, with attractive rooms
with bathroom, TV, phone and a/c. There's a decent cheap
restaurant downstairs and it's cheaper off season (**E**).
Closed November.

Camping
Camping Bahía de la Plata, Carretera Atlanterra s/n,
T 956 439 040. *1.5 km south of Zahara's centre.* A shady spot
with plenty of trees on the beach. It's open year round and can
organize a variety of summer watersports. There are also
bungalows available for hire.

Bolonia

There are many places to stay and eat, nearly all closed in winter.
D **Hostal Lola**, Calle El Lentiscal 26, **T** 956 688 536. A fine
option with decent, well-looked-after rooms and very
welcoming owners.

Tarifa and around

L Hotel Arte Vida, Carretera N 340, Km 79.3, **T** 956 685 246, www.hotelartevida.com. *Playa de los Lances, 5 km north of town. Map 6, H6, p257* This beautiful hotel is one of the best upmarket options on Playa de los Lances. Painted red and grey, it's attractively and quirkily decorated. Rooms lead out onto an inviting grassy terrace overlooking the ocean and have very large beds, wooden floors, esparto blinds and a decent bathroom. The restaurant is excellent, with a startling array of dishes from around the world (including a delicious Vietnamese beef salad), plenty of vegetarian options and great views over the ocean.

L Hurricane Hotel, Carretera N340, Km 78, **T** 956 684 919, www.hotelhurricane.com. *6 km north of Tarifa. Map 6, H6, p257* This beachside hotel is a deserved favourite, situated in a peaceful leafy garden. Although the rooms, the more expensive of which face the beach, are somewhat overpriced in summer (but **A** in winter), the hotel's facilities are excellent, including swimming pool, internet, gym, a bar and a pool table. There's also an attached kite- and windsurfing school (see below) as well as horse stables and bikes for rental. Breakfast is included in the price, and you can have meals in the restaurant and the beach bar.

AL La Sacristía, Calle San Donato 8, **T** 956 681 759, www.lasacristia.net. *Map 5, E5, p256* Pleasingly refurbished 17th-century building in the heart of town, ideal for a relaxing stay. There's a distinctly Japanese feel to the decor; the rooms are simply but very attractively furnished, with massive never-get-up-again beds, tasteful lamps, floor mats, antique chairs and objets d'art, heating and fine bathrooms. The most attractive is on the top floor, an attic-like apartment under the dark wooden roof. Downstairs there's an enticing lounge with a fireplace, and some meals can be arranged (breakfast is included). Live guitar music some evenings.

B Casa Amarilla, Calle Sancho IV El Bravo 9, **T** 956 681 993, **F** 956 627 130. *Right in the heart of town.* Map 5, E5, p256 An excellent apartment-style hotel with refreshing art nouveau and North African interiors and top light, comfortable and elegant rooms equipped with kitchen which offer very good value compared with other Tarifa options; it's cheaper off season (**D**). Recommended.

B Hostal Tarik, Calle San Sebastián 34, **T** 956 680 648. *Map 5, B1, p256* A reasonable option near the sea, with clean comfortable rooms that are light and airy opening off a streetside balcony. The owners are friendly and well used to windsurfers (**D** off season).

B Hotel La Mirada, Calle San Sebastián 41, **T** 956 684 427, www.hotel-lamirada.com. *Map 5, B1, p256* This has cheerful rooms with nautical blue and white striped bedcovers, heating, TV and clean, modern bathrooms. Pleasant and welcoming, with breakfast available downstairs, this is a likeable option near the sea (**D** off season).

C Hostal El Asturiano, Calle Amador de los Ríos 8, **T** 956 680 619. *Just outside the Puerta de Jerez.* Map 5, C4, p256 This large building is run by amicable Asturians (ask at the bar if they've got any bottled *sidra* in stock). The rooms are typical for this town, standard airy spaces, slightly overpriced in summer but with a relaxed beachy air.

E Hostal Africa, Calle María Antonia Toledo 12, **T** 956 680 220, hostal_africa@hotmail.com. *Just inside the Puerta de Jerez.* *Map 5, D3, p256* This excellent budget choice is on a quiet old-town street. The rooms, which come with or without bath, are warmly welcoming, painted in attractive colours, and with seriously comfortable beds; there's also a roof terrace. The young owners are lively and welcoming; they can store boards or do washing. Recommended.

F Casa de Huéspedes Eusebio, Calle Amador de los Ríos 1 (no phone). *Directly opposite the Puerta de Jerez.* *Map 5, C3, p256* This place offers value with its very basic but clean rooms around a faded patio. Curious but good-hearted management.

Rooms and apartments
There's a large range of apartments and *casas rurales* available for weekly rent both in and around Tarifa; the tourist office can give (or email) you a full list.

Huerta Grande, Pelayo s/n, **T** 956 679 700, www.huertagrande.com. *15 mins' drive east of Tarifa in the Parque Natural Los Alcornocales. Map 6, H6, p257* A very peaceful complex of *casas rurales*. There are wood cabins as well as refurbished country houses, all well equipped and rentable as complete buildings or per room. The furniture is beautifully wooden and rustic; there are verandas for enjoying the sun, fine views, and a swimming pool and restaurant on the site.

The Secret Garden, **T** 609 565 953. *On the hillside above Playa de los Lances. Map 6, H6, p257* Run by Iris, a charming Greek lady who has fitted more into her long life than would fill this guidebook. This is two cottages each with modern kitchen and bathroom, as well as a veranda with peaceful views over the ocean. They sleep four and are sheltered from the easterlies by the hills behind. Good walking, and not far from the beach.

Camping
There are several campsites near Tarifa, strung out along Playa de los Lances.

Camping Tarifa, Ctra N340, Km 78, **T** 956 684 778. *Near the Hurricane Hotel by the beach. Map 6, H6, p257* Has good facilities, including rental apartments. Open all year.

Río Jara, Ctra N340, Km 80, **T** 956 680 570. *4 km from town. Map 6, H6, p257* The closest to town and a relaxed spot; you can hire horses here.

The supreme culinary achievement of this part of Spain is, of course, *tapas*. The word refers to barfood served in saucer-sized portions typically costing €1-2. The best idea is to go to several bars, trying tapas and having a drink in each one, but you can also stay put and order larger portions, known as *raciones*. Although the quality of the tapas is usually high, an eye for what the locals are ordering will further elevate the experience, as each bar is normally known for something they do especially well.

On the tapas crawl, people drink wine or beer. Spanish lager is good, but you should certainly at least try the local dry sherries and *manzanillas*, great accompaniments to seafood.

Lunch is the biggest meal of the day for most people in Spain and it's also the cheapest time to eat a full meal. Just about all restaurants offer a *menú del día*, which is a three-course meal with various choices that includes wine or soft drink. Expect to pay €6-10 for a standard place. Most places open for lunch at about 1300, and stop serving at 1500 or 1530, although at weekends this can extend.

Cádiz

Cádiz has some excellent seafood restaurants. The area around Plaza de la Mina, especially Calle Zorilla, is good for tapas, as is the Paseo Marítimo in the new town.

Restaurants

¶¶¶ **El Faro**, Calle San Félix 15, **T** 956 229 916. *Daily 1300-1600, 2000-2400. Map 1, G4, p250* This whitewashed little place with a row of tavern lamps outside looks like a humble enough spot at first glance, but is actually one of the region's most celebrated fish restaurants, and deservedly so. The menu and wine list are excellent; some recommendations include *rape con pasas y jerez* (monkfish stewed in raisins and sherry), any of the rice dishes, and the *paté de cabracho*, a tasty scorpionfish mousse. There's a tapas bar where you can enjoy cheaper but equally perfect fare.

¶¶ **El Balandro**, Alameda Apodaca 22, **T** 956 220 992, *Tue-Sun 1200-1700, 1900-2400. Map 1, A6, p250* A large and sophisticated seafood restaurant and tapas bar with a comfortable dining area looking out across to the bay. The

121

fresh local fish is very tasty, as are the salads, and the prices very reasonable for the quality on offer. At the bar there's very courteous service and fine wines by the glass among the busy buzz of upmarket *gaditanos*.

₩ **Puntaparrilla**, Glorieta de Cortadura s/n, **T** 956 201 332. *Tue-Sun 1300-1700, 2000-0100. Right at the end of the Paseo Marítimo, almost at the edge of the city. Map 1, F12, p251* One of the city's best options for a meaty meal. Classy place which does excellent roasts and grills in massive portions.

₩ **Freiduría Las Flores**, Calle Brasil s/n and Plaza de Topete 4, **T** 956 289 378. *Daily 0900-1630, 2000-2400 or later. Map 1, F12 (off map), p251 and Map 1, D6 p250* A Cádiz institution, with locations in the old and new towns. What they do is fried seafood, and they do it exceptionally well and cheerily. A mixed bag costs €4 for a quarter kilo to take away and munch on the beach; you can also graze on tapas at the bar or sit down for larger portions.

₩ **Gotinga**, Plaza Mentidero 15, **T** 856 070 580. *Corner of C Hércules. Mon-Sat 1300-0130. Map 1, B3, p250* A warm and welcoming little restaurant with cool yellow walls. They do tapas but really focus on a handful of fresh fish and pasta dishes, which are prepared with tender loving care. The menu ranges across various countries, including such inventive fusions as pork with tsatziki. There's plenty of veggie choice, and they mix a fine cocktail too.

₩ **Mesón de las Américas**, Calle Ramón y Cajal 10, **T** 956 224 410, *Daily 1200-1600, 2000-2400. Map 1, B8, p251* This appealing Argentinian restaurant is definitely not for claustrophobes, with its narrow, vaulted, underground dining area, but for good food at sharp prices it's a great bet. Big salads cost a mere €4, while mains range from cheap plates of meat 'n' sauce to large steaks such as *bife de chorizo* (€10). At street level is a bar for wine and tapas.

Tapas bars

🍴 **Arte Serrano**, Paseo Marítimo 2, **T** 956 277 258. *Daily 1100-2400. Map 1, F12, p251 (off map)* In an unmistakable building on the beachfront promenade, this is one of Puerta de Tierra's most visited spots. Inside the massive but warm space, you can sit down and enjoy the seafood or browse the very extensive tapas menu standing at the long bar. Tapas range from €1.50 to €2.50 and all are delicious.

🍴 **Taberna San Francisco I**, Plaza San Francisco 1, **T** 956 212 597. *Daily 0930-0200. Map 1, B6, p250* An upmarket red-ceilinged corner bar built in stone and brick with an inviting wooden terrace on the square. There are original *raciones* such as moussaka served on outsized white plates; there are also mixed platters typical of various regions of the province, several vegetarian options, and a good but pricey wine list. If you're not a salt-lover, tell them to ease off when you order your food.

🍴-🍴 **Mesón Cumbres Mayores**, Calle Zorilla 4, **T** 956 213 270. *Daily 1230-1630, 2030-2400. Map 1, A5, p250* This ultra-atmospheric spot is as good as it ever was, and is one of Andalucía's most lovable tapas bars. It oozes character from its wooden beams, lively range of customers, hanging ham and garlic. The staff are on the ball, and will recommend from their long tapas list. *Diablillos* (dates wrapped in bacon), the pork *secreto* or a *carrillada* are all worth trying. It's also a fine place to sit down and eat, with efficient service at the tables out the back. The mixed grill for two showcases Huelva's finest pork products and is a bargain at €15.65, while the salads are a refreshing complement. Highly recommended.

🍴 **Bahía**, Avenida Ramón de Carranza 29, **T** 956 281 166. *Mon-Sat 1100-1700, 1900-2300, Sun 1100-1700. Map 1, B8, p251* One of the Cádiz classics, this is the best of a short string of bars opposite the passenger docks near the tourist office. It's famous among locals for its pork ribs and fish in saffron sauce, and also has a shaded terrace outside and as-it-should-be service.

Casa Taberna Manteca, Calle Corralón de los Carros 66, **T** 956 213 603. *Tue-Sun 1100-1600, 1900-2300. Map 1, F4, p250* One of the city's favourite tapas bars, this lively spot is decked out top to bottom with photos of flamenco and bullfighting. The tapas are all *chacinas* (hams, sausage, cured pork, cheeses), and are served on squares of greaseproof paper. The ham melts like butter in the mouth and the service is keen and friendly. Locals nod knowingly when you mention this bar around Cádiz.

Casa Tino, Calle Rosa 25, **T** 956 214 313 *Tue-Sat 1200-1630, 1900-2400, Sun 1130-1830. Map 1, E4, p250* A small and neatly fitted bar with bright lights and hanging onions, pictures of horses and black and white photos of Cádiz personalities. The tapas to try here are seafood and stews; the latter fill a range of metal pans sitting temptingly on the bar. Among the fishy offerings, try the fresh *ortiguillas* from the bay.

La Gorda te da de Comer, Calle General Luque 1. *Tue-Sat 1300-1600, 2100-0100, Mon 2100-0100. Map 1, B7, p251* A busy and friendly bar with chatty staff, brightly painted walls, wooden tables and a touch of the 60s thrown in. *La Gorda* (the fat lady) turns out to be the gay chef, and he turns out generous tapas of typical Cádiz dishes for a pittance, around €1.20. The daily specials are always tasty and innovative; the proof of the pudding is that not many tapas bars have queues outside waiting for opening time!

La Nueva del Puerto, Calle Calderón 1, **T** 956 211 573. *Tue-Sun 1100-1600, 1900-2330. At the bottom of Calle Zorilla. Map 1, A5, p250* This unsophisticated bar has a great atmos-

★ **Weird and wonderful tapas**

- Marinated cubes of shark (*cazón*) at Freiduría Las Flores, Cádiz, p122
- Dates wrapped in bacon (*diablillos*) at Mesón Cumbres Mayores, Cádiz, p123
- Bulls' balls (*criadillas*) at Casa Balbino, Sanlúcar de Barrameda, p129
- Grilled sweetbreads (*mollejas*) at El Reino de León, Jerez de la Frontera, p135
- Sea anemones (*ortiguillas*) at El Nani, Barbate, p139

phere with its chessboard tiles, barrels and cheerful standing crowd. The prawn beer taps give a handy clue to the bar's speciality; the fried fish and *montaditos* are other reliable choices. The beer is very cold, as it should be; there are also a few tables for a larger feed.

Cafés
El Tendero, Avenida Ramón de Carranza 24, **T** 956 261 349. *Mon-Sat 1000-2300. Opposite the port. Map 1, C8, p251*
A cheerful and warm café which does a powerful coffee and a range of pastries and croissants. Converts itself seamlessly into a popular evening tapas bar specializing in ham.

La Catedral, Plaza de la Catedral 9, **T** 956 252 184. *Daily 1030-2400. Map 1, E8, p251* A fine spot to sit on a fake wooden terrace in a pretty square with palm trees beneath the looming façade of the cathedral. Despite the location, it's far from a tourist trap, with high-quality tapas also available, as well as full meals.

La Morería, Calle San Pedro 5, **T** 856 170 323. *Mid-Jun to mid-Sep Mon-Fri 1900-late, mid-Sep to mid-Jun Sun-Thu 1600-2400, Fri and Sat 1600-0300. Map 1, B6, p250* Long, narrow and atmospheric Moroccan-style *tetería*, with many different teas as well as fresh juices. It gets lively at weekends with traditional dancing and other Moroccan cultural events.

El Puerto de Santa María

El Puerto is a very inviting place to eat. The **Ribera de Marisco** near the ferry dock has a string of simple and excellent seafood eateries, including the legendary Romerijo. There are some excellent tapas bars in the streets behind the Ribera de Marisco. It's popular to duck across from Cádiz on the boat for a boozy outdoor lunch.

Restaurants
¶¶¶ El Faro de El Puerto, Carretera Fuentebravía Km 0.5, **T** 956 858 003. *Daily 1300-1600, 2100-2300. Map 2, H1, p252 (off map)* Established by the same owners as El Faro in Cádiz, this elegant gardened mansion just outside town showcases the finest of Spanish seafood in refreshingly different ways. You might want to try the black rice with squid and cuttlefish, a lighter dish of red mullet with aubergine, or the utterly sensuous carabineros in oloroso sherry. The service is faultless and wine list good.

¶¶ Rajamura, Calle Micaela Aramburu 28. *Mon-Sat 1200-1630, 2000-2300. Map 2, G5, p252* A contrast to the big-portioned meat and seafood spots around the waterfront, this newly opened restaurant specializes in a more delicate and imaginative cuisine. Still leaning heavily on seafood, the menu features such delights as carpaccio of salmon and prawns.

¶¶ **Romerijo**, Ribera de Marisco s/n, **T** 956 541 254. *Daily 1100-2400. Map 2, C5, p252* A legend in its own lunchtime, these simple eateries are basically just outdoor terraces with metal tables and buckets for the prawn shells. Their reputation rests solely on the high quality of the seafood. One of the eateries specializes in frying, one in boiling, and both have takeaway outlets. At the tables, *surtidos* (mixed plates) feed two and cost from €8.25 up to €55 for the deluxe version. Recommended.

Tapas bars

¶ **El Artesano Leonés**, Calle Luna 4, **T** 956 859 636. *Thu-Tue 1200-1600, 2000-2400. Map 2, D5, p252* An atmospheric spot near the waterfront, filled with deli products and delicious cured meats from the fascinating northern province of León. Try the *cecina*, a delicious 'beef ham', and accompany it with a red wine from El Bierzo, a full-bodied aromatic drop that hasn't achieved the fame in Spain that it perhaps deserves.

¶¶ **Taberna Manzanilla**, Calle Ribera del Río s/n. *Tue-Sun 1130-1630, 1900-2330. Map 2, B5, p252* Just along from the *Ribera del Marisco* is this likeable little stone place with its wooden beams and barrels of good *manzanilla* and moscatel. It's particularly popular at weekends, when there's an in-house seafood stall and folk happily munching away on all sorts of tasty creatures.

¶ **La Andana**, Calle Misericordia 9, **T** 956 870 922. *Wed-Mon noon-1600, 1900-2330. Map 2, B5, p252* Behind the seafood strip is this little street, well stocked with quality tapas bars. This spacious example has a long bar and a fine variety, including excellent cured meats, stews and tripe. At the tables you can eat more elaborately, and there are several vegetarian choices.

¶ **La Bodeguilla del Bar Jamón**, Calle Misericordia 5,
T 956 850 322. *Tue-Sun 1200-1630, 1900-2300. Map 2, B5, p252*
Another reliable option, this bar is at its busiest on Sundays,
when, at precisely 1430, the star tapa is unveiled, a delicious
seafood rice. Be there promptly, as the hungry hordes tuck in
and it has a tragically short lifespan. At other times, there's good
berza (pork and vegetable stew) and big *panes* (open sandwiches).
Photos of frighteningly large porkers overlook proceedings.

Sanlúcar de Barrameda

The best spot is **Bajo de Guía**, where a row of seafood restaurants
with terraces overlooking the rivermouth cater to every budget.

Restaurants
¶¶¶ **Casa Bigote**, Bajo de Guía s/n, **T** 956 362 696. *Mon-Sat
1200-1630, 1900-2400, closed Nov. Map 3, A5, p253 (off map)*
The *sanluqueño* restaurant with the most formidable
reputation. It maintains very high standards, and a meal
on the terrace by the beach won't be forgotten in a hurry, unless
you overindulge on the *manzanilla*. There's efficient service and a
fine range of fresh seafood. House specialities include *langostinos*
(king prawns) and *raya* (skate). The paella, too, is a thing of
excellence. Recommended.

¶¶ **La Lonja**, Bajo de Guía 8, **T** 956 383 642. *Tue-Sun 1200-1700,
1900-2400. Map 3, A5, p253 (off map)* Another reliable seafood
terrace overlooking the beach and the water. Try 200 g of *navajas*
(razor shells) washed down with *manzanilla*, then tackle a seafood
rice for two (€15) while enjoying the sunshine!

¶¶ **Paco**, Chipiona, within the port complex, **T** 956 374 664.
Tue-Sun 1300-1700, 2000-2400. Map 6, D3, p257 A place for a
serious seafood meal; the chef buys his fish direct from the boats

outside so they are deliciously fresh. Just take the recommendation for whatever's good that day.

☗ **Casa Ballén**, Calle Banda Playa 9. **T** 956 381 792. *Mon-Sat 1200-1630, 1900-2300. Map 3, D5, p253* This cheap and cheerful local is the spot where workers go for lunch; always an good sign. There's a top value *menú del día* for only €5.90, also available in the evenings. They also do good fried fish platters, among other things.

Tapas bars

☗☗ **Cantina**, Calle Infanta Beatriz 2, **T** 956 360 742. *Daily 1100-1600, 1900-2330. Map 3, E3, p253* Despite being part of an ugly hotel and Guinness-free 'Irish' pub complex, this tapas bar manages to rise above its station. At tables in an attractive low wine cellar you can enjoy fine *raciones* and very generous tapas. The *solomillo* is excellent – you can have it with a variety of sauces – there's also seafood on offer. For a rich treat, you can't ignore the quail stuffed wlth foie. Service is very good here.

☗☗ **Casa Balbino**, Plaza del Cabildo 11. T 956 362 647. *Daily 1100-1700, 1830-2400. Map 3, F3, p253* An excellent tapas bar, one of Andalucía's most memorable, and resolutely taurine with a couple of bull heads on the walls and numerous pictures. There's an outside terrace too (no table service). The friendly and extremely energetic staff will have your *manzanilla* on the bar before you've even asked. The tapas here are excellent; there's a wide range including tasty stuffed potatoes, but you'd be a fool not to try some seafood.

☗ **Bar Clemente/Juanito**, Plaza San Roque s/n. T 956 368 137. *Tue-Sun 1100-1600, 1830-2330. Map 3, G4, p253* A friendly bar with a small terrace on this interesting square. The tapas are really excellent, including several types of prawns, sea snails and tasty *ensaladilla*. Around midday, it's full of locals grumbling about football and politics.

Cafés
Heladería Bornay, Plaza del Cabildo 2, **T** 956 362 213. *Daily 1000-2200. Map 3, F4, p253* This café and ice creamery is a Sanlúcar institution and over a century old. Now with many branches around town, this is still the best spot to sit, on the terrace right in the heart of the action.

Coto Doñana

Mazagón

Restaurants
¶¶ **El Remo**, Avenida de los Conquistadores 123, **T** 959 536 138. *Thu-Tue 1300-1630, 2000-2400. Right on the beach, 1 km or so along from the centre* Tasty *raciones* of fried fish in its summer *chiringuito* as well as more formal seafood (which they take seriously!) in an elegant dining area. The grilled meats are a tasty alternative to the fish. Usually closed for one or two months between October and December.

¶¶ **Las Dunas**, Avenida de los Conquistadores 178, **T** 959 377 811. *Summer daily 1300-1600, 2000-2400, winter Tue-Sun 2000-2400, also Fri and Sat 1300-1600. At the bottom of the Av de la Playa where it hits the beach in the centre of town.* This excellent seafood establishment specializes in whole grilled fish; the seafood rice dishes are also memorable. There's a big outdoor terrace to enjoy them.

Tapas bars
¶ **Bar Cipri**, Plaza Trainera s/n, Aptos Sol y Mar 1, **T** 959 536 254. *Wed-Mon 1000-1600, 1900-2300. Situated on the small plaza tucked behind the Café Paris on the main road.* Although it's unprepossessing in appearance, with its white padded sofas, this polished wooden bar guards high-quality tapas; try the mussels.

🍴 **Bar El Choco**, Avenida Fuentepiña 47, **T** 959 536 253. *Tue-Sun 0800-1600, 1900-close.* A cheerful spot on this bar-clad street, with a marine-coloured awning marking a sunny terrace, and an interior lined with photos of old fishing adventures. There's all manner of fried seafood at good prices, including *raciones* of *ortiguillas* (sea anemones) or *huevas de merluza* (hake roe); unusual things that taste much better than they sound.

🍴 **Las Redes**, Avenida Fuentepiña 17. **T** 959 376 960. *Wed-Mon 1100-1700, 1930-close. On the main pedestrian street.* One of several options serving cheap *raciones* and tapas, this good-hearted bar is known for its *revueltos* (scrambled egg dishes, €8) and good-value *menú del día* (€7). If the wind's given you a chill, go for the warming *cazuela tío Diego* stew, otherwise seafood is a reliable fallback.

Cafés
Andévalo, Avenida de la Playa 24. *Daily 1600-0100, closed Nov.* A quiet little café-bar run by a friendly local with a pronounced Sheffield accent. There's a sunny conservatory area, and it's a good place to enjoy a peaceful coffee or an after-dinner *cubata*.

Matalascañas

🍴🍴 **Casa Matías**, Parque Dunar s/n, **T** 959 449 809. *Tue-Sun 1200-1700, 1900-close.* On the roundabout by the tourist office, this large building is impossible to miss and is the town's most welcoming restaurant. The interior is typically Andalucían, with whitewashed walls and wooden beams; the bar does a wide selection of tapas and the restaurant offers such appetizing choices as *almejas al ajillo* (clams sizzling in garlic) or hake croquettes.

El Rocío

Restaurants

🍽 **El Pastorito**, Calle El Ajoli 177, **T** 959 442 186. *Daily 1200-2300, closed during the Rocío festival. A couple of blocks north of the large central park.* This relaxed terraced bar outdoes itself in providing hungry visitors with high-quality grilled meat as well as a few seafood dishes. The service is friendly and relaxed, so hitch your horse to the rail and tuck in!

🍽 **Toruño**, Plaza del Acebuchal s/n, **T** 959 442 422. *Wed-Mon 1100-1630, 1900-close.* You won't go hungry in the town's best restaurant, opposite the hotel of the same name (see Sleeping, p105); the staff seem determined to put a bit of meat on your bones. The place is deceptively large; the main dining area has a great view over the marismas and their bird and horse life. There's a wide selection of meat and fish dishes here, including the best of Huelvan pork.

Lugares Colombinos

Palos de la Frontera

Apart from the hotel restaurants (see Sleeping), there are several tapas bars scattered along the main street.

🍽 **El Paraíso**, Calle Rábida 117, a block down the street from the Hotel La Pinta. A comfortable outdoor terrace and very tasty fresh grilled fish with rock salt.

Moguer

Few eating options but fortunately there are two good recommendations.

¶¶ **La Parrala**, Calle Fray Andrés de Moguer 22, **T** 959 370 452. A smart place with excellent grilled meats.

¶ **El Lobito**, Calle Rábida 31. Ultra-characterful and in sharp contrast to Moguer's elegant whitewashed lanes. Customers scribble on the walls, the ceiling hangs with all kind of weird and wonderful curios, and the kitchen trucks out decent fish and meat grills as well as tapas.

Jerez de la Frontera

Jerez has some excellent restaurants and tapas bars; many of the dishes use sherry, which is also often drunk here as an accompaniment to a meal.

Restaurants

¶¶¶ **La Mesa Redonda**, Calle Manuel de la Quintana 3, **T** 956 340 069. *Mon-Sat 1300-1700, 2000-2400. Map 4, A8, p255* An established and traditional Jerez restaurant which has gained a well-deserved reputation for itself. Local cuisine including, of course, several tasty meat dishes in some sort of sherry sauce. Try a *caldereta* if it's on; these stews are completely delicious.

¶¶ **Bar Juanito**, Calle Pescadería Vieja 4, **T** 956 334 838. *Summer Mon-Sat 1100-1630, 1900-2330, winter Tue-Sat 1100-1630, 1900-2330, Sun 1130-1800. Map 4, G5, p255* One of Jerez's classics, this is a place that must be visited during your stay. With a small bar, large covered patio for dining, and a beautiful terrace shaded by white cloth, it's a welcoming spot, and the quality of the food is sky-high. Ask the barstaff what they recommend that day; suggestions include *carrillada*, prawns, *berza* or *calamari*, washed down of course with a selection from a long list of sherries.

♜ **La Cepa de Oro**, Calle Porvera 35, **T** 956 344 175. *Tue-Sun 1230-1630, 1900-2330. Map 4, D5, p254* A fine cosy place popular with all sorts of people and open for years. The homestyle cooking is the big attraction; this is the sort of spot to try classic Andalucían dishes such as *berza* (a spicy stew of beans, sausage and cumin), *potaje de alubias con chorizo* (hearty bean stew, a Jerez classic) or *rabo de toro* (bull's tail). There's a small terrace on the lively street.

♜ **Parrilla la Pampa**, Calle Guadalete 24, **T** 956 341 749. *Summer Mon-Sat 1300-1600, 1900-2330, winter Thu-Tue 1300-1600, 1900-2330. Map 4, B5, p254* A big barn of a place, this is an Argentinian meat restaurant; the tables are already set with steak knives, and the walls decorated with cowhides, snakeskins and photos of the pampas. The best value here are the excellent mixed platters for two, but all the meat is tasty, as are the *empanadas* and the desserts using *dulce de leche*, the sweetened condensed milk that South America is understandably addicted to. Be warned, if you ask for your steak rare (*poco hecho*), that's exactly how it will come.

♜ **Tendido 6**, Calle Circo 10, **T** 956 344 835. *Mon-Sat 1200-1630, 2000-2400. Map 4, B9, p254* Despite the garish neon sign, this is a classy restaurant. Opposite the bullring, there's no prizes for guessing the main theme of the decor, but it's a warm comfortable spot with fine service. The meat is good, but there's also excellent fish, such as *urta*, a popular local variety of bream. There's a tapas bar attached.

♕-♕ La Carboná, Calle San Francisco de Pula s/n, **T** 956 347 475. *Wed-Mon 1300-1600, 2000-2400. Map 4, G8, p255* A cavernous restaurant set in an old sherry bodega and beautifully atmospheric. Usually busy for the fine quality of its grilled meats (try the *chuletón* if you're hungry) and very reasonable prices. Everyone, from sherry baron to student, enjoys it here.

♕ El Reino de León, Calle La Torre 8, **T** 956 322 915. *1100-1600, 1900-2330. Map 4, G5, p254* This unassuming restaurant tucked away behind the Plaza del Arenal appears very unremarkable but is quite a find. You get a free tapa with your drink, but it's worth ordering more, or sitting at a table and having a full meal. The *mollejas* (sweetbreads) are a delight and worth coming for alone. Other worthwhile dishes are *cecina* (cured beef) or just about anything else. The prices are very reasonable.

Tapas bars

♕ Café La Moderna, Calle Larga 65. *Daily 1000-2400. Map 4, E6, p254* As down to earth as you can get in central Jerez, this popular bar/café is always lively and has an excellent atmosphere. The back room is lovely, with wooden beams and brick vaulting up against a section of the old city walls. There are also simple filling tapas available, such as stews of beef, venison or tripe (*menudo*). The beer is cheap too.

♕ Cervecería Gorila, Plaza Plateros s/n, **T** 654 383 904. *Mon-Sat 1100-1700, 1830-0100. Map 4, F5, p254* A cheerful spot for a drink or a bite to eat. The beer is remarkably cold and refreshing; there are several varieties on tap, and if there are a few of you (or you're thirsty), you can order a three-litre keg that's insulated to keep the stuff icy. There are tasty *montaditos*, and various larger dishes that you can eat upstairs; these include German sausage and cheese platters.

❢ **El Gallo Azul**, Calle Larga s/n, **T** 956 326 148. *Mon-Sat 1200-1600, 1900-2400. Map 4, F6, p254* Right in the heart of things, this fine tapas bar and café is set in an unmistakeable rounded brick building dating from the early 1900s which used to be a famous meeting place for Jerez intellectuals. There's a good restaurant on the 1st floor (❢❢), but the greatest pleasure here is to have a *fino* in its narrow bar or on the terrace, and pick from some of the fine cold seafood canapés at the counter.

❢ **La Abacería**, Plaza Rafael Rivero s/n. *Tue-Sun 1200-1600, 1900-0100. Map 4, D5, p254* This small square has a handful of popular tapas bars, including this attractively decorated wooden grocery bar, which specializes in ham, sausage and cheese tapas, but has also achieved fame for its anchovies. You can sit on the terrace outside too.

❢ **Tabanco San Pablo**, Calle San Pablo 12, **T** 956 351 401. *Tue-Sun 1030-1600, 1900-2300. Map 4, H6, p254* A very authentic bar, where the sherry barrels are not for decoration but consumption. It's an old-fashioned Spanish spot with yellowing bullfight posters on the walls; the sherry is served in humble glasses and doesn't taste any the worse for it. There's not a big range of food, but the *montaditos* are sensational, especially the ones with *chorizo*.

White towns of Cádiz

Arcos de la Frontera

Restaurants
❢❢ **El Convento**, Calle Marqués de Torresoto 7, **T** 956 703 222. *Daily 1230-1630, 2000-2400.* Run by the same owners as the hotel of the same name, this lovable restaurant is set in a 17th-century palacio with an elegant patio to dine around. There's a wide

selection of meats, including many game dishes; the *albóndigas* (meatballs) are very tasty, as is the *choco a la plancha* (grilled cuttlefish). Don't miss the rich, butterscotchy *tocinillo de cielo* for dessert.

Tapas bars
♟ **Mesón de Lola**, Calle Boticas 7, **T** 956 701 807. *Tue-Sun 1000-1600, 1830-2300.* With colourful pictures on the walls and a relaxed friendly atmosphere, this is one of the town's better tapas bars. The beer is served refreshingly cold and usually comes with a free tapa to accompany it. The bar does great cold potato and egg *aliños*, as well as tasty meat stews and battered prawns.

Medina Sidonia

Restaurants
♟ **Restaurante Machín**, Plaza de Iglesia Mayor s/n, **T** 956 411 347. *Daily 1100-1630, 1830-2330.* A top place to eat opposite the church at the top of this white town. It's got a dining area and terrace with fine views across the countryside below. There's a *menú del día* for only €7, and other traditional dishes such as rabbit in garlic or *arroz a la cazuela*, a simple, tasty rice dish.

South from Cádiz

Conil de la Frontera and El Palmar

There are good seafood restaurants on the Paseo Marítimo in Conil. Heading up from here, the Plaza Santa Catalina has more bars and restaurants. Calle Hospital has many more tapas bars; passing these on the way to La Fontanilla are some very local bars which will cook up fish for you.

Restaurants

🍴 Casa Francisco, Paseo Marítimo s/n, El Palmar, **T** 956 232 786. *Daily 1000-2330.* You can't miss this sturdy tavern in the hamlet of El Palmar; it's the main place to stay, have a coffee, or eat and does all in style. The restaurant specializes in fish baked in salt, which is unbelievably succulent and juicy. All the seafood is of the highest quality and freshness, and the prices are very reasonable for what's on offer.

🍴 El Timón de Roche, Avenida Inglaterra, Roche, **T** 956 446 232. *Tue-Sun 1300-1700, 1900-2330.* A few kilometres north up the coast from Conil is the residential complex and beach of Roche. It's a nice strip of sand, and here is one of the better restaurants in the province. A romantic spot, with the sea, sand, and setting sun, it calls for, and delivers, fine seafood. The waiters will tell you proudly of Pierce Brosnan's visit when he was filming a 007 flick in Cádiz.

Tapas

🍴 El Gamba, Plaza Santa Catalina s/n, Conil. *Mon-Sat 1100-1530, 2000-0100.* Right opposite the Torre de Guzmán is this ivy-covered bar and restaurant. It's popular with visitors for its terrace in the pretty square as much as for its high-quality swordfish and *mojama*, the cured tuna typical of the region.

🍴 Bar Los Hermanos, Plaza Puerta de la Villa s/n, Conil, **T** 956 412 309. *Dec-Oct Tue-Sun 1000-1600, 1830-2330.* Just near the arch that marks the top of the old town, this simple bar is the locals' favourite destination for fried fish, which are delicious as a tapa or *ración*.

Cafés

Café de la Habana, Plaza Santa Catalina s/n, Conil, **T** 956 443 484. *Daily 1030-0130.* This relaxed place is a popular Conil meeting point at any time of day. In the morning you can enjoy a *tostada* with the traditional *manteca colorá* spread; there's also a wide selection of teas and infusions. In the afternoon scrumptious cheesecakes appear, while later on people take advantage of the Cuban theme by sipping *mojitos* or other cocktails.

Los Caños de Meca and Cabo Trafalgar

Restaurants
♟ **El Mero**, Carretera Zahora-Los Caños s/n. **T** 956 437 308. *Nov-Sep daily 1100-2300.* A hostal with a friendly restaurant. Excellent whole fresh fish cooked in the house style with plenty of crisped garlic costs only €9.50, and there's a cheap *menú del día*. It's on the main road 3 km north of Los Caños de Meca in the village of Zahora.

♟ **El Pirata**, Avenida Trafalgar 67, **T** 956 437 396. *Daily 1200-0200. Town centre.* A cosy spot perched on the low cliffs above the beach. It's got great views, is open year round and serves up tasty seafood-based dishes for €6-12. After eating hours, it's also the area's best pub, with frequent live music.

Barbate

Restaurants
♟♟ **El Nani**, Paseo Marítimo s/n, **T** 956 453 133. *Mon-Sat 0900-2300, Sun 1130-1800.* The best of the string of seafood eateries along the beach promenade. You can take away portions of fried fish, or sit on the terrace and enjoy the freshest of fresh at knockdown prices, with a big plate of mackerel (*caballas*) only €5, and grilled tuna €9.

♟♟ **Estrella Polar**, Avenida Generalísimo 106, **T** 956 433 304. *Wed-Sun 1200-1700, 1900-2330.* Another reliable seafood choice, favoured by locals for its *tortillitas de camarón* (thin fried shrimp omelettes). Appetizers include *ortigas* (sea anemones) and large salads, while the fish depends on what's been caught. The *pargo* (sea bream) is reliably delicious, and the oven-baked *mero* (grouper) with clams is another gem.

Cafés

Cafetería Juan José, Avenida Andalucía s/n, **T** 956 431 780. *Daily 0900-2400*. The place for breakfast in Barbate. Work up an appetite by strolling around the food market opposite, then come in here for the quiet elegance, friendly service and strong coffee. The *tostadas* are typical, and come with a choice of spreads such as pâté or *manteca*.

Vejer de la Frontera

Restaurants

♥♥♥♥ **La Vera Cruz**, Calle Eduardo Shelly 1, **T** 956 451 683. *Thu-Tue 1300-1630, 2000-2400*.This is a very classy restaurant set in a 16th-century chapel. There are creative and fine fish and seafood dishes such as *mero al whisky* or prawn salad with pastis, as well as excellent *retinto* beef, wild boar pâté and scrumptious desserts. There's a feast of a *menú* for €20 at weekday lunchtimes.

♥♥ **El Jardín del Califa**, Plaza de España 21, **T** 956 451 706. *Mid-Sep to mid-Jun daily 1300-1530, 2000-2330, mid-Jun to mid-Sep Mon-Sat 1330-1600, 2030-midnight, Sun 2030-2400*.
This amazingly atmospheric place is one of the best places to eat, reached via a series of stairs in the Casa del Califa hotel. There's a variety of intimate nooks to eat, as well as a garden and an open pavilion. The food is fantastic, with a North African/Lebanese bent. There are many vegetarian options available and the prices are very reasonable.

♯ **Casa Rufino**, outside town, in the village of La Muela, **T** 956 448 481. *Daily 1300-1630, 2000-2400. 2 km off the main road opposite Vejer.* An excellent *venta* with cheap and filling local Andalucían cooking. The *potajes* (stews) are particularly good and, if the weather's fine, you can eat on the terrace. You may have to wait for a table at weekends, as it's a popular excursion for folk from Cádiz.

♯ **Mesón El Palenque**, Calle San Francisco 1, **T** 670 641 579. *Tue-Sun 1300-1630, 2000-2330. On a small plaza by the market.* Another cheap option with outside seating. There are various meat and seafood raciones between the €5 and €10 mark, and a good selection of *platos combinados* for around €5. Good value.

Zahara de los Atunes

In summer, you can't beat the *chiringuito* on the beach next to the Hotel Gran Sol, which doles out tasty *raciones* of fried seafood to its busy terrace.

Restaurants
♯♯♯ **Bar Ropiti**, Calle María Luisa 6, **T** 956 439 344. *Tue-Sun 1230-1630, 1900-2330.* A fine lunch or dinnertime choice with a cool covered patio; they do good tuna steaks and *carpaccios* and also specialize in *caracoles de mar* (sea-snails), which are very tasty with a dash of lemon. The service is particularly good here.

♯ **La Botica**, Calle Real 13, **T** 956 438 183. *Wed-Mon 1200-1700, 1900-2300.* An honest and inviting restaurant and tapas bar, decked out in wood and jute, with hanging hams and bags of garlic. The *revueltos* (scrambled egg dishes) are tasty, and if you're hungry you can go to town on *cochinillo al horno* (roast sucking pig); the seafood is also delectable.

♟ **La Jabita**, Calle María Luisa 20. **T** 956 439 595. *Tue-Sun 1900-0100.* A cheerful place to eat, with such windsurfer comfort foods as fondue or lasagna, as well as fine salads and sandwiches. It's also one of the livelier spots in town to head for a drink later on.

Bolonia

Restaurants
♟ **La Cantina**, El Lentiscal 2, Bolonia, **T** 956 688 624. *Daily 1200-1600, 1900-2300.* A relaxed, open-air wooden restaurant set back a little from the beach. There's tasty wood-fired pizza as well as grilled meats; it's also a spot for a drink, with table football as well as slide and swings for the kids.

Tarifa and around

There's a huge range of eating choice in Tarifa during summer, and places are constantly coming and going. In winter far fewer spots are open. Along Playa de los Lances, one of the best is in the Hotel Arte Vida (see Sleeping, p115), while in town there are traditional Spanish options, an assortment of international cuisines and various windsurfer comfort spots with traveller-fusion cuisine and plenty of vegetarian choice.

Restaurants
♟♟ **Iris' Manau Greek Taverna**, Calle San Sebastián 10, **T** 956 627 408. *Tue-Thu 2000-2400, Fri-Sun 1300-1600, 2000-2400. Map 5, C2, p256* Although it may be closed by the time you read this, as the incredibly engaging Greek lady running it was thinking of selling up, you're in luck if it's still open. Authentic and delicious Greek cuisine, as well as fine ouzo and retsina to wash it down with. The best way of eating here is to order a *mezze*, a large selection of small dishes; the onion and octopus *stifado* is sensational, as are the *dolmades* and taramasalata. Highly recommended.

★ **Fish restaurants on this coast**

Best

- El Balandro, Cádiz, p121
- El Faro de El Puerto, El Puerto de Santa María, p126
- Casa Bigote, Sanlúcar de Barrameda, p128
- Casa Francisco, El Palmar, p138
- Bar Ropiti, Zahara de los Atunes, p141

♈ Morilla, Calle Sancho IV El Bravo 2, **T** 956 681 757. *Daily 1100-1700, 1900-2330. Opposite the church. Map 5, D5, p256*
This warm and busy restaurant is one of the town's best places to enjoy succulent fresh fish and typical *gaditano* dishes. The boss is friendly if a little pushy, but be sure to check prices before taking recommendations on the day's tastiest catch.

♈ Souk, Calle Mar Tirreno 46, **T** 956 627 065. *0900-2330. Tough to find, it's 3 blocks back from the beach about 1 km from the centre. Map 5, F1, p256* An attractive and romantic basement restaurant devotedly and charmingly decked out in North African style. The shortish menu is mainly Moroccan, although it adds several Thai and Indian curries to fill things out. The atmosphere is great, the food average, and the service friendly! Upstairs, the café serves a range of delicious teas and snacks.

♈ Vaca Loca, Calle Cervantes s/n. *Daily 1800-0100. Map 5, E4, p256* Tucked away in the heart of old Tarifa, this attractive wood and stone bar is a popular evening destination. It can feel a bit touristy, but people keep coming for the outdoor tables, where sizzling offerings from the BBQ are served: steaks, sausages, brochettes, and the like, ranging from €8-13 per plate.

Eating and drinking

Tapas bars

It's worth investigating Calle Guzmán El Bueno, where there are some good little options seldom visited by tourists.

ᵞ¶-ᵞ Café Central, Calle Sancho IV El Bravo 10, **T** 956 668 056. *Daily 0900-2400. Map 5, D5, p256* A fine standby at any time of the day, this is Tarifa's most venerable café at more than a century old, and a long-established meeting point in the heart of town. Cold fresh beer, a sunny terrace, tempting tapas and well-priced fresh fish dishes; not a bad combination in anyone's language.

ᵞ Café Continental, Paseo de la Alameda s/n, **T** 956 684 776. *Tue-Sun 1000-2300. Map 5, E3, p256* A quiet and amicable spot with tasty lunchtime tapas and hearty coffee. They sometimes have live music in the evenings and there's a sunny terrace out on the alameda. A good place for an early evening drink or to relax with a decent novel.

ᵞ El Picoteo, Calle Mariano Vinuesa s/n, **T** 956 681 128. *Wed-Mon 1100-1600, 1900-2400. Map 5, G1, p256* If you tire of trendy Tarifa's international feel and long for a good honest Spanish bar, this is the place for you. Friendly, warm, and typical, it's always full of locals snacking on the bar's tasty tapas or dining on stews, seafood, and grilled meats. Excellent value.

Andalucía's nightlife is excellent, particularly in summer, when lively beachside *chiringuitos* and *discotecas* cater for the crowds that flock to the coast. All the cities have fine year-round action, particularly Cádiz. Late night bars are known as *bares de copas* or pubs; and the action (*la marcha*) doesn't usually hit them until after midnight, when people have stopped eating. Many of these bars, and clubs (called *discotecas*) are only open from Thursday to Saturday nights, although you'll always find a busy bar somewhere during the week. *Discotecas* are often away from the centre of town to avoid council restrictions on closing hours. They tend to fill up from 0300 onwards, and many are open until well after dawn. You won't find cutting-edge dance music in these places; the standard mix is a blend of Spanish pop (particularly from *Operación Triunfo*, the amazingly successful popstar-creation TV show), international hits, and a kind of techno/pop mix known as *bacalao*. Other places will have a more latino slant, with salsa and merengue music.

Cádiz

Bars

Cádiz has excellent nightlife year-round. In summer, the focus is on the beach, while for the rest of the year it's around Plaza San Francisco, moving to Punta San Felipe later on. This pier jutting into the bay has many bars as well as the city's best *discoteca*. In Plaza San Francisco itself there is a lively and friendly *botellón* scene on Thursday to Saturday nights, driven mostly by students. Several shops in the surrounding streets sell drink, so join the party and meet some locals! In the new town, the Paseo Marítimo beyond Calle Brasil has many bars, as does Calle General Muñoz Arenillas. On the beach in summer are numerous *chiringuitos* which pump their music late and loud.

Barabass, Calle Muñoz Arenillas 4, **T** 856 079 026. *Daily 1700-late, admission free. Map 1, F12, p251 (off map)* With chill-out music in the evenings turning into house beats later on, this stylish pre-club venue with dark stone tiles and slick modern decor gets packed at weekends. There's a door policy but it's not cliquey, and is one of the better places for a drink on Sunday night. Usually open until 0500 or so.

Carbonera, Calle Marqués de Cádiz 1, **T** 956 272 800. *Mon-Sat 1100-1600, 1800-2300. Map 1, D9, p251* This sort of bar is a disappearing breed in Spain, replaced by more fashion-conscious watering holes. This could define the word authentic, with its faded tiles, weathered old men and barrels of simple, tasty and cheap *finos* and *manzanillas*; an exercise in simplicity.

El Pay-Pay, Calle Silencio 1, **T** 956 252 543. *Tue-Sat 2130-0200 or later, admission varies but usually free or a pittance. Map 1, E10, p251*

Once an elegant society café, then a high-class brothel, this place has recently been reopened as a bar and music venue. There are frequent live shows, ranging from flamenco to comedy to jazz and blues, as well as exhibitions of photos and paintings. Whatever's on, there are always plenty of people drinking in the characterful interior until late.

Memphis, Avenida Amilcar Barca 35, **T** 956 252 423. *Daily 1200-0100, later at weekends, admission free. Map 1, F12, p251* On the beachfront, this is a big lively *cervecería* with a terrace. Nearly always busy, there's plenty of comfortable seating and a pool table; it's also a popular local spot to watch football. Part of the same complex is a Caribbean-themed *discoteca* open from midnight until 0500 at weekends.

Persígueme, Calle Tinte s/n, between Plaza de la Mina and Plaza San Francisco. *Thu-Sat 2200-late, admission free. Map 1, B6, p250* This long dark spot with two bars fills up at weekends with interesting people in the mood for drinking and dancing. A good pre-*discoteca* option; there's sometimes live music on offer.

Woodstock, Calle Canovas del Castillo, **T** 956 212 163. *Tue-Sun 2000-0200. Map 1, B6, p250* A cosy wood-lined bar in the old town that is an unremarkable but reliable spot for a drink. The music tends towards classic rock, and there's an enormous variety of bottled beer to choose from. There's another branch on the Paseo Marítimo in the new town, which is less intimate but boasts great beach views from its large windows.

Clubs

La Punta/Sala Anfiteatro, Punta San Felipe s/n. *Thu-Sat 2400-0700, admission €8. Map 1, A7, p251 (off map)* Cádiz's best *discoteca* is at the end of the Punta San Felipe strip that juts into

★ **Antidotes to chain pubs**

Best

• Carbonera, Cádiz, p147
• El Pay-Pay, Cádiz, p147
• Chanca, El Palmar, p154
• La Pequeña Lulú, Los Caños de Meca, p155
• Janis Joplin, Vejer de la Frontera, p154

the bay. It is, in fact, an amphitheatre in shape, and gets busy around 0300-0400 until closing time at 0700. Entry can be tricky on Saturday night, so it's worth turning up early to beat the crowds. The cover includes a drink. Music is light dance to Spanish pop hits, and usually better on Saturday than Friday; there are also go-go dancers who are a cut above the average. In the same strip are many disco-bars.

El Puerto de Santa María

There are several bars in the streets behind the Ribera de Marisco, but in summer head to Playa de Valdelagrana, which is one long raucous strip of nightlife, with *chiringuitos*, pubs and *discotecas* galore. The in places change every summer, so just head down and see where it's all happening.

Bars

Café de Aquitania, Calle Luna 7, **T** 656 485 308. *Mon-Wed 0830-2300, Thu-Sat 0830-late. Map 2, D5, p252* A sleek and friendly bar decorated in pastel shades and black and white photos. It's a relaxed spot for a coffee or a drink; be sure to check out the cute colourful toilets. Mixed crowd.

Clubs

El Niño Perdío, Bajada del Castillo 1, **T** 956 586 489. *Nightly 2300-0600. Map 2, F5, p252* The Puerto's busiest and most reliable nightspot, the 'Lost Boy' is a cheerful disco-bar playing hits from the latest Spanish pop idols amid a cheerful throng downing generous mixed drinks.

Sanlúcar de Barrameda

Bars

The best zone for bars is the grid of streets around Carril San Diego and Calle Santa Ana. There are several *discobares* around here.

Café Sonoro, Paseo Marítimo s/n. *Tue-Sun 1800-0200. Map 3, A5, p253 (off map)* A trendy new bar in Bajo de Guía, just along from all the fish restaurants. Stylish and polished, it's become one of the town's favourite weekend options.

Kábala, Calle Diego Benítez s/n. *Tue-Sun 2000-0200. Map 3, F5, p253* A friendly place for a quieter drink, decorated with astrological symbols and strategically placed witches. There are several board games, and the bar serves the cheerful Portuguese lager *Superbock*.

Coto Doñana

Mazagón

Bongo, Avenida Santa Clara 4. *Daily in summer 1000-late, Thu-Sun only in winter*. A lively late-opener with trendy native American and African decor. In winter it's a cosy bolthole frequented by locals, while in summer, outdoor drinking buzzes every night on the pavement under the brush awning.

Cotton Club, Plaza Trainera s/n. *Open daily in summer 1000-late, Fri-Sat only in winter*. Mazagón's main year-round *discoteca* is tucked away on a plaza behind the Café Paris. It throngs with all-comers in summer, but is still reliable for a dance and a drink any given weekend.

Matalascañas

Coto's, Avenida de las Adelfas s/n. *1900-late*. One of many bars in the strip running from the tourist office towards the beach; but you can't miss Coto's, with its striking thatched roof. It's an unsubtle good-time sort of place with plenty of varieties of beer and atmosphere that ranges from cheery to riotous depending on the season.

Lugares Colombinos

Moguer

Cister, Calle Fray Andrés de Moguer 16. This big bar is right opposite Santa Clara. During the day it can seem a little cavernous with its brick arches and high wooden roof, but it gets going after dinner with the sound system up and a good percentage of Moguer's young dancing at weekends.

El Lobito, see Eating, p133, is a drinker's bar too.

Los Leones, Avenida Andalucía 2, just off Plaza Cabildo, which plays rock in a grungy atmosphere until late at weekends.

Jerez de la Frontera

Bars

Jerez's nightlife is generally very quiet and it can be difficult to find a busy bar midweek. The main nightlife area at weekends is along Avenida de Méjico, which is a youngish scene and has a big range of bars and discobars. Mangú is currently a popular choice for dancing, while Kangaroo has nothing Australian about it apart from a tin roof and some dodgy Aboriginal murals, but is busy with an interesting pre-club crowd.

Don Juan, Calle Letrados 2, **T** 956 343 591. *1800-2400. Map 4, F5, p254* You couldn't get much more Jerez than this elegant little bar. The low-polished wooden furniture and polite, well-fed proprietor attract a dressy young to middle-aged set for quiet drinks and chat.

Duplicado, Plaza Vargas 2, **T** 956 326 329. *Map 4, F5, p254* A beautifully decorated bar, attractively done out in wood and brick with hanging musical instruments. There's a friendly bohemian clientele, with a high gay and lesbian element.

El Rincón del Pirata, Calle Divina Pastora s/n, **T** 956 321 600. *Open nightly 2000 till late, admission free. Map 4, A6, p254* One of the more atmospheric bars on this street, serving good shooters and cocktails in a tropical ambience, with a large and deadly rum selection. There's occasional karaoke.

La Plaza de Canterbury, Calle Zaragoza s/n, **T** 696 958 128. *Daily from 2000 and earlier, admission free. Map 4, B8, p255* Not just a single bar, but an enclosed square near the bullring, surrounded by several lively drinking bars. It's particularly animated in summer, when everyone's sitting outside.

Los Dos Deditos, Plaza Vargas s/n, **T** 956 326 452. *Open nightly 2000-0100, admission free. Map 4, F5, p254* This spacious pub has walls decorated all over with pictures of beer, as if you didn't know why you were there in the first place. It's a very attractive spot that's been one of the city's favourite drinking destinations for years. They pour a good *Guinness* and there's also the fine beer German *Paulaner* on tap.

Clubs

Grafton Street, Calle Zaragoza s/n, **T** 656 958 128. *Corner of C Nuño de Cañas. Thu-Sun 0100-0700, admission €8 including drink. Map 4, C8, p255* A lively *discoteca* with a lightly worn Irish theme. Popular with a mid-20s to 30s crowd; the music ranges from Spanish pop hits to light techno. **Enigma**, opposite, is a more dance-music oriented place, a darker spot with strobes and a younger trendier clientele.

White towns of Cádiz

Arcos de la Frontera

Círculo de la Unión, Calle Boticas 6, **T** 956 703 107. *Daily 1130-1700, 1830-2300*. Set in a small square off the main street, opposite Mesón de Lola, the attraction of this bar is its terrace, an unbeatable spot to enjoy a drink in the blazing sunshine.

Vejer de la Frontera

La Bodeguita, Calle Marqués de Tamaron s/n, **T** 956 451 582. *Daily 1100-2400*. A fine friendly sort of a bar with wooden arching over the bar, a dark and cosy place. Outside is a small terrace covered by grapevines, a great place to sit nursing a beer and watcing the world go by. The bar also does decent tapas.

Janis Joplin, Calle Marqués de Tamarón 6. *Daily 2130-0300*. A well-known bar that attracts people from all over the region. The decoration is beautiful, a sumptuous neo-Moorish flight of fancy, and the music (mainly rock 'n' roll) and company always reliably good. It's so good, people come from Cadiz, a city which already has several great bars.

South from Cádiz

Conil de la Frontera and El Palmar

Chanca, Paseo Marítimo s/n, El Palmar, on the road, **T** 659 977 420. *About 500 m south of Casa Francisco. Daily 1100-0100*. This excellent place is a sort of ultimate *chiringuito* and one of the best spots on the coast for a drink. It's got a big garden with hessian parasols shading the tables, all of which look directly out over the water. It's the perfect spot for a refreshing something while watching the spectacular sunset. It's also an upmarket spot to eat, with a few tables bearing the weight of some seriously good seafood rices.

Los Caños de Meca

La Pequeña Lulú, Avenida de Trafalgar 2, **T** 956 437 355. *Winter Thu-Sun 1300-0300, summer daily 1300-0300.* Relaxed by day, modish by night, and never less than interesting. The beachfront road ends here, at this cute bar which is the destination of plenty after a day on the beach. There's nowhere better to sit in town than the terrace with sea and sky around; at night the interior pumps with the resident DJ's sounds. You can also snack here; the crêpes are particularly tasty.

Tarifa and around

Tarifa's nightlife is distinctly seasonal, in summer much of the action centres around the *chiringuitos* on the beaches and the latest ephemeral *discoteca*; off season the bars in the old town are quiet but constant companions.

Bars

Misiana, Calle Sancho IV El Bravo 18, **T** 956 627 083. *Daily 1800-2400. Map 5, D4, p256* This bar under the hotel of the same name has been given a trendy new refit and is all colourful designer furniture and strategically placed neon lamps. An in place for an evening drink, but doesn't stay open nearly as late as the set-design suggests.

Nogal, Calle San Francisco 10. *Daily 2100-0200. Map 5, E4, p256* A small and quiet cave-like locale in the old town. It's likeably chaotic, with wine bottles perched on protruding tiles and flickering candles. Among other things, they do tasty *mojitos* and *caipirinhas*.

Clubs

La Jaima, Playa de los Lances s/n. *Wed-Sat 0130-0700. Map 5, H1, p256 (off map)* Famed for its summer nights, this big Moroccan tent is right on the beach and fills with a happy dancing crowd. The music is mainly house and other upbeat seaside sounds.

Rif, Calle Batalla del Salado s/n. *Jun-Sep daily 0100-late, Oct-May Thu-Sat only. Map 5, A1, p256* One of the better *discotecas* in town, opposite the petrol station on the way into town from the north. A variety of music from dance to international pop, and sometimes live flamenco on Thursdays.

While at first glance this coastal paradise might seem to offer more to the surfer than the culture vulture, a closer look will reveal plenty to get excited about. Cádiz, with its liberal traditions, is a stronghold of the arts, and has a reputation for its theatre and music. The annual Carnaval provides ample opportunity for the expression of artistic talent!

Andalucía is the cradle of flamenco, and the Costa de la Luz has some important centres, particularly Jerez de la Frontera. Although usually associated with the tweed jackets of the sherry industry, the city also has a sizeable gypsy community, who have traditionally lived in the fascinating barrio of Santiago, where you'll find several character-laden venues. Another town with a flamenco culture that is alive and well is Vejer de la Frontera and Lebrija.

Cinema

Nearly all foreign films shown at cinemas in Spain are dubbed into Spanish (*doblada*); a general change to subtitling is strongly resisted by the acting profession, many of whom have lucrative ongoing careers as dubbers for a particular Hollywood star. Entrance to cinemas is typically about €4-6; there's often a 'cheap day' (*día del espectador*), usually a Tuesday or Wednesday. When a film is shown subtitled, the term is *versión original* (vo).

Cádiz

Multicines Bahía de Cádiz, Avenida Cortes de Cádiz 1, **T** 956 256 212. *Map 1, F12, p251 (off map)* Further into the new town.

Multicines El Centro, Plaza de Palillero s/n, **T** 956 808 106. *Map 1, C6, p250* Handiest to the centre.

El Puerto de Santa María

Cine Macario, Calle Luna 16, **T** 956 871 193. *Map 2, D4, p252* Historic cinema in this summer resort, recently refurbished in faux 18th-century style.

Jerez de la Frontera

Multicines Abaco, Centro Comercial Jerez Norte, Avenida de Europa s/n, **T** 956 304 470. *Map 4, p254 (off map)* A large multiplex on the edges of town.

Tarifa and around

Cine Alameda, Calle Colón s/n, **T**956 680 994. *Map 5, D3, p256* An offbeat, old-style cinema next to Tarifa's food market.

Flamenco

Whether you're planning to spend every hour of darkness trawling bars in search of the most authentic *cante jondo* or just want to briefly experience what it's all about, it's likely that you'll want to see some flamenco while you're here. Nearly every town will have some sort of venue, but the best place to go is Jerez de la Frontera, and the atmospheric gypsy barrio of Santiago. While much of what's on offer is geared to tourists (although frequently of a very high technical standard), it's still possible to track down a more authentic experience. Larger, theatre-style performances are in venues known as *tablaos*, which typically charge €10-25 for drink and show and are touristy. Some of the best flamenco evenings can be had in *peñas de flamenco*. These are social clubs formed by aficionados of the art and generally put on weekly shows in small bars. They are private clubs, so you may be refused entry, but if you show a genuine interest you'll usually be let in. A couple of general rules: don't talk during the performance unless locals are and don't clap in time even if locals are.

Cádiz

La Cava, Calle Antonio López 16, **T** 956 211 866. *Map 1, A7, p250* Has a fairly good flamenco show on Thursdays. It's quite a dressy spot. Entry to the show is €21; this includes a drink.

Sanlúcar de Barrameda

A Contratiempo, Calle San Miguel 5, **T** 653 071 099. *Map 3, H2, p253* Live flamenco on Friday and Saturday nights at 2330 and 0030. Thursdays see fusion-flamenco, while on Wednesday there are flamenco and salsa classes.

Jerez de la Frontera

Jerez is an important centre of flamenco and you can find both the touristy dinner-and-packages as well as classy performances in smoky bars. The best place to find out about upcoming performances is the Centro Andaluz de Flamenco (see p74); the newspaper *Jerez Información* also has a flamenco page.

There are many *peñas* and flamenco bars; some of the most authentic include:

El Garbanzo, Calle Santa Clara 9, **T** 956 337 667. *Map 4, H6, p254* Regular performances, both scheduled and unscheduled.

El Lagá de Tío Parrilla, Plaza del Mercado s/n, **T** 956 338 334. *Map 4, E2, p254* Although there are plenty of tourists, the flamenco here is often of very high quality. Daily shows at 2230 and 0030; entry free, but drink prices are steeper than normal.

La Bulería, Calle Mariñíguez 15, **T** 956 323 468. *Map 4, H9, p255* Another likely spot to find something good at the weekend.

South from Cádiz

Peña Cultural Flamenca Niña Barbate, Plaza Carlos Cano, Barbate.

Peña Cultural Flamenca, Calle Rosario 29, Vejer de la Frontera, **T** 956 450 017. A dark and cavernous bar, an atmospheric place that often holds weekend flamenco performances.

Zoco Flamenco, Calle Juan Relinque 28, Vejer de la Frontera **T** 609 176 103. Another popular venue.

Galleries

Cádiz

Sala Rivadavia, Calle Presidente Rivadavia 3, **T** 956 211 269.
Map 1, B5, p250 Exhibitions of contemporary paintings and
sculpture.

Isla Habitada, Calle Sacramento 24, **T** 956 213 457. *Map 1, D5,
p250* Stylish modern gallery displaying work by local artists.

Sala Caja San Fernando, Avenida Ramón de Carranza 26,
Map 1, C9, p251 **T** 956 272 966. Bank-sponsored local gallery.

Jerez de la Frontera

Sala Caja San Fernando, Calle Larga 56, **T** 956 597 100.
Map 4, F6, p254 Regular changing exhibitions.

Sala Pescadería Vieja, Calle Pozuelo s/n, **T** 956 337 306.
Map 4, F5, p254 There's usually something interesting or different
on here.

South from Cádiz

Sala Municipal de Exposiciones, Avenida de la Playa s/n, Conil
de la Frontera, **T** 956 440 911. Usually concentrates on local artists.

Music

The main venues for classical concerts are the theatres (see below). For live music, see also the Bars and clubs section, and the flamenco section above.

Cádiz

El Pay-Pay, Calle Silencio 1, **T** 956 252 543, *Tue-Sat 2130-0200 or later, admission varies but usually free or a pittance.*
Map 1, E10, p251 Once an elegant society café, then a high-class brothel, this place has recently been reopened as a bar and music venue. There are frequent live shows, ranging from comedy to jazz and blues, as well as exhibitions of photos and paintings. Whatever's on, there are always plenty of people drinking in the characterful interior until late.

South from Cádiz

Sala Fussion, Calle Santa Angela de la Cruz s/n, Chiclana, **T** 610 540 391. Relaxed café-bar with live music nearly every weekend, typically modern fusion jazz or flamenco.

Theatre

There are theatres in almost every medium-sized town upwards. They tend to serve multiple functions and host changing programs of drama, dance, music and cinema. There are often only one or two performances of a given show. Tickets are very cheap by European standards.

Cádiz

Central Lechera, Plaza Argüelles s/n, **T** 956 220 628. *Map 1, A6, p250* In the old central dairy, this is a likeable venue for theatre and comedy.

Gran Teatro Falla, Plaza de Falla s/n, **T** 956 220 894. *Map 1, D3, p250* The main venue for theatre and music in town in an elegant neo-*mudéjar* setting in the heart of the old city.

Jerez de la Frontera

Teatro Villamarta, Plaza de Romero Martínez s/n, **T** 956 329 313. *Map 4, F6, p254* Jerez's main venue for theatre, music and dance performances. Dress up if you want to be inconspicuous.

White towns of Cádiz

Teatro Olivares Veas, Calle Olivares Veas s/n, Arcos de la Frontera, **T** 956 703 013. Arcos' main theatre, with more on in summer than in winter.

Even the smallest village in Spain has a fiesta and some have several. Although mostly nominally religious in nature, they usually include the works: a Mass and procession or two to be sure, but also live music, bullfights, competitions, fireworks and copious drinking of *calimocho*, a mix of red wine and cola (not good, but not as bad as it sounds).

Although the daddy of all festivals on the Costa de la Luz is Carnaval time in Cádiz, a celebration of exuberance and carefully honed wit (see box), most fiestas are during the summer. It's always worth asking around if there's something on, as it is impossible to list all the fiestas of smaller villages here.

While visiting a local fiesta is one of Spain's unmissable experiences, these can be difficult times to travel; it's important to reserve travel in advance to avoid queues and lack of seats. If the holiday falls mid-week, it's usual form to take an extra day off, forming a long weekend known as a *puente* (bridge).

January

Cavalcada de los Reyes Magos (night of 5 January)
The three kings parade through the streets in colourful horse-carriages, tossing sweets and gifts to onlookers.

February

Carnaval (28 February 2006, 20 February 2007, 5 February 2008) There are Carnaval celebrations in all towns and villages, but the Cádiz knees-up (see box, p168) is the biggest event. The main day is Shrove Tuesday, forty-seven days before Easter Sunday, and the weekend before it. Other places where it gets lively are Tarifa, El Puerto de Santa María, and Sanlúcar de Barrameda.

Festival de Flamenco (late February and early March)
The main flamenco festival of the Costa de la Luz region takes place in Jerez de la Frontera and is centred on the Teatro Villamarta (see p164).

March/April

Semana Santa (20-27 March 2005, 9-16 April 2006, 1-8 April 2007, 17-24 March 2008) The famous Easter processions of Sevilla, with their *pasos* of Christ and the Virgin carried through the city streets by hooded *nazarenos* and cross-carrying *penitentes* are reproduced on a lesser scale in many towns and cities. In the Costa de la Luz, the most notable processions are in Jerez de la Frontera and Sanlúcar de Barrameda, while in Arcos de la Frontera the floats are specially customized to negotiate the narrow streets.

Carnaval de Cádiz

Cádiz has always half faced away from Spain, out to sea, and it's no surprise that the carnival there is very different to those of the rest of the peninsula.

Part of this can be ascribed to the independent *gaditanos* themselves, and part to the extensive contact and interchange Cádiz enjoyed with cities such as Venice and Genoa.

The party in Cádiz goes for nine days, although it centres on Shrove Tuesday. Everyone dresses up in some sort of fancy dress and takes to the streets for much drinking and merriment. There's plenty of live music and other performances, but the most famous come from the *agrupaciones*, groups of musicians and comedians who satirize contemporary political figures and events. The best-loved are the *chirigotas*, choirs of 10 singers accompanied by guitar, bombo and a wooden box used as a drum. Their songs are usually the most biting and

sung to popular folk tunes. During the week, these groups, as well as roaming the streets, compete for a prestigious prize in the Gran Teatro Falla. There are plenty of impromptu musical gatherings on the streets too, whether it be flamenco or some of Cádiz's more exotic rhythms such as samba or a creole beat. There are several parades, and a daily ear-splitting explosion of firecrackers in Plaza San Juan de Dios known as *La Toronda* (the thunderclap).

It's very difficult and expensive to get accommodation in Cádiz over Carnaval. It should be booked several months if not longer in advance. Even nearby cities like El Puerto de Santa María are usually full. If you can't get a bed, it's not a big deal. Plenty of people stay up all night and then get the train back to Jerez or Sevilla, only to return for the next night's festivities. The atmosphere on this 'party train' can be colourful in itself.

May

Feria de Primavera (late April and early May) El Puerto de Santa María celebrates its spring festival, with parades, bullfights, and hedonism.

Feria del Caballo (1-8 May 2005) Jerez's main fiesta runs for a week, starting on the first or sencond Sunday of the month. It's a riot of colourful flamenca costumes and families and friends parading in horse carriages. Private *casetas* (stripy tents) are used to entertain, but there are also many public ones. It's also the time when the city's best bullfights are scheduled. The motorcycling Grand Prix is usually within a week or so of the Feria, and sometimes during it, which stretches the city to bursting point.

Feria de la Manzanilla (end May) Sanlúcar de Barrameda has a dressy fiesta similar to that in Jerez earlier in the month. It celebrates the town's winemaking tradition by consuming as much as possible of the stuff.

May/June

Romería del Rocío (16 May 2005, 5 June 2006) The annual pilgrimage to El Rocío (see box, p59). It's also a busy time in Sanlúcar de Barrameda, as many of the brotherhoods gather in Bajo de Guía to be ferried across the river.

July

Espárrago Rock A rock festival in Jerez that pulls some big national and international names. The month has a history of varying.

August

Horse races (1, 2, 3, 16, 17, 18 August 2005) Sanlúcar de Barrameda races along the sands (see p51).

Fiesta de Nuestra Señora de la Caridad (13-15 August) Sanlúcar de Barrameda fiesta, where the local Virgin is carried through the streets in procession over colourful patterns made from dyed salt crystals.

Velada de Agosto (mid-August) Vejer de la Frontera kicks off for a two week celebration.

Noche Flamenca (mid-August) A flamenco festival in Vejer de la Frontera. A similar evening takes place in Barbate in August as well.

September

Nuestra Señora de la Luz (5-13 September) This is Tarifa's major bash for the year.

Feria de San Miguel (29 September) The big day of the year in Arcos de la Frontera, when bulls with padded horns are let loose in the streets. The locals run before them, dodging into doorways and jumping up on street signs and balconies to evade them.

October

La Virgen del Rosario (7 October) Cádiz celebrates its patron saint.

San Dionisio (9 October) Jerez de la Frontera celebrates its patron saint. Around this date, the Fiestas de Otoño are a month of cultural activities.

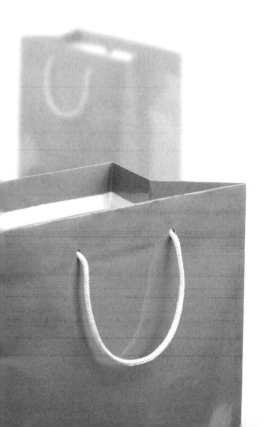

Although Spain has not wholly resisted the chain-store curse, one of the most endearing aspects of the country is the profusion of small shops, many little changed in recent decades and always family run. While supermarkets are two a penny, there are still plenty of bakers too; people buy their newspapers from kiosks, their tobacco from tobacconists, and they get their shoes repaired at cobblers'. And food markets are still the focus of many towns.

Andalucía is famous for its handicrafts, many of which developed in Moorish times. Pottery, leather goods, marquetry, textiles and wickerwork are all relatively cheap and widely available in craft shops and markets. It's best to buy the *artesanía* from the town or village where it is produced. Local fiestas usually have one or more handicrafts markets attached to them; these can be excellent places to shop, as artisans from all around the region bring their wares to town; you'll soon distinguish the real ones from the samey stalls selling imported South American trend items and pseudo-Jamaican knicknacks.

Spain's not as cheap as it used to be, but it's still a good place to shop. Clothing is an obvious one; Spanish fashion is strong and not overly influenced by the rest of Europe. While the larger Spanish fashion chains have branched out into Britain and beyond, there are many smaller stores with good ranges of gear that you won't be able to get outside the country. Cádiz and Jerez de la Frontera are the spots to head for.

Another obvious choice is food and drink. The Costa de la Luz is famous for its seafood preserves; Barbate is the place to go, while it'll be hard to resist taking home a bottle from the home of sherry!

Nearly all shops close for the siesta. Standard hours in this part of the world are: Monday to Friday 1000-1400, 1700-2000, and Saturday 1000-1400.

Books

Quorum, Calle Ancha 27, Cádiz, **T** 956 807 026, *Map 1, C6, p250*
A central bookshop with a range of maps, travel literature, and books in English.

Crafts

Artesanía Alboreá, Calle Nuestra Señora de la Oliva 7, Vejer de la Frontera, **T** 956 451 629. *Winter Mon-Sat 1030-1400, summer*

Mon-Sat 1030-1400, 1700-2000. Fabrics, ceramics, and other crafts next to the Iglesia del Divino Salvador.

Arx-Arcis, Calle Marqués de Torresoto s/n, Arcos de la Frontera, **T** 956 703 951. A pleasing art gallery and shop, with traditional Andalucían handcrafts such as colourful tiles.

El Boliche, Calle Mesón 2, Cádiz, **T** 956 254 972. *Map 1, E9, p251* One of the Barrio del Pópulo's several good craft shops, with imported Moroccan fabrics and other bright things.

Galería Artesanal El Pópulo, Calle San Antonio Abad 12, Cádiz. *Map 1, E10, p251* A series of craft shops tucked into a little passageway in the heart of the Barrio del Pópulo. The shops here include **Edén**, with some breathtakingly beautiful handpainted fans.

Pangea, Plaza San Martín 3, Cádiz, **T** 956 280 697. *Map 1, E9, p251* Set in a beautiful building in the Barrio del Pópulo; an old admiral's house, this gallery and ecological shop has storage pots still in place underfloor.

Sinfín, Calle Batalla del Salado 22, Tarifa, **T** 956 627 087. *Map 5, B2, p256* A trendy spot on Tarifa's main drag, with accessories, puzzles, pop-art chic, lamps, clothing, and even cans of Tarifa air.

Tierra Artesanía, Calle Rosario 12, Cádiz, **T** 956 229 050. *Map 1, B7, p251* An attractive gift shop near Plaza San Francisco, with Moroccan-inspired handicrafts and materials.

Department stores

El Corte Inglés, Avenida Cortes de Cádiz 1, Cádiz, **T** 956 297 100. *Map 1, p251, off map* Spain's premier department store, with almost anything you could want to buy.

Fashion

Aldea Global, Calle Batalla del Salado 7, Tarifa, **T** 956 685 272.
Map 5, C3, p256 A big and colourful surfwear shop which also has
its own T-shirt designs.

Bershka, Calle Lancería 9, Jerez, **T** 956 168 492. *Map 4, G6, p254*
A cheap and cheerful Spanish fashion store for girls that are young
or young at heart.

Cortefiel, Avenida Andalucía 64, Cádiz, **T** 956 274 158. *Map 1,
F12, p251 (off map)* Classic, elegant, fashion for ladies of all ages,
but with more to offer in the 30 plus ranges.

El Tamboril, Calle Las Carretas 3, El Rocío, **T** 959 442 703.
A branch of a famous Sevilla shop specializing in typical fiesta and
rociera fashion, much of it designed to look good atop a horse. You
can't miss the tiled front.

Mango, Calle Columela 23, Cádiz **T** 956 213 206. *Map 1, C7, p251*
Massive but cool Barcelona-based chain peddling fashion to trendy
young ladies.

Stradivarius, Calle Larga 3, Jerez, **T** 956 339 880. *Map 4, F6, p254*
Fashion *provocativo* for women of 15-30 or anyone who likes to
flaunt it a little.

Women's Secret, Calle Columela 32, Cádiz, **T** 956 221 934,
and Calle Larga 30, Jerez, **T** 956 335 307. *Map 1, E7, p251*
and *Map 4, F6, p254* A good shop for lingerie, underwear,
bikinis and pyjamas.

Zara, Calle Feduchy 6, Cádiz, **T** 956 222 802, and Calle Honda 5, Jerez, **T** 956 345 911. *Map 1, E7, p251* and *Map 4, E6, p254* With several branches in both cities, this international chain offers elegant rags in a fairly Spanish style. The label has been successful in Britain and elsewhere; there's more variety to be had here, and also lower prices.

Food and drink

Bodegas La Gitana, Banda de la Playa 24, Sanlúcar de Barrameda, **T** 956 385 304. *Map 3, F3, p254* One of many bodegas where you can buy the local *manzanilla* sherry.

Conservas y Salazones La Barbateña, Avenida Generalísimo 142, Barbate, **T** 956 434 323. *Map 6, G5, p257* The millennia-old tradition of salting and preserving fish is alive and well on this coast. This shop-exhibition on the edge of Barbate has a range of excellent products, including pretty jars of such delights as tuna balls in sherry, or hake roe in olive oil.

La Casa del Jerez, Calle Divina Pastora 1, Jerez, **T** 956 4. *Map 4, B7, p255* Somewhat touristy, but still has a fine selection of sherries to take home.

Maype, Calle Corneta Soto Guerrero 3, Cádiz, **T** 956 214 652. *Map 1, C8, p251* The whole of Spain munches the marzipan confections made in Cádiz, and this traditional Spanish patisserie is a great place for the sweet of tooth to stock up.

Ultramarinos Barreda, Calle San José 1, Cádiz, **T** 956 212 703. *Map 1, B5, p250* Just off Plaza de la Mina, this is a typical old Spanish grocery store of a type that is fast being killed off by supermarkets. There are tinned delicacies (Spanish canned food is a class above its British counterpart) and sweets from all parts of the country; it's worth entering just for the atmosphere.

Markets

Mercadillo del Pópulo, Cádiz. *Map 1, E9, p251* Quirky flea market held in the characterful barrio of El Pópulo on the third Saturday of every month.

Mercado de Abastos, Avenida Andalucía s/n, Barbate. *Mon-Sat mornings*. *Map 6, G5, p257* Small but lively food market is a good example of the traditional place to buy the daily necessities in a Spanish town.

Market days around the province include: **Arcos de la Frontera** (Friday), **Chiclana** (Tuesday), **Jerez** (Monday), **El Puerto de Santa María** (Tuesday), **Sanlúcar de Barrameda** (Wednesday).

Music

El Carbonero, Calle San Miguel 14, Jerez, **T** 956 336 797. *Map 4, H6, p254* Sells fabulous handmade guitars.

JM, Calle Columela 16, Cádiz, **T** 956 211 226. *Map 1, E7, p251* Calle Medina 24, Jerez, **T** 956 341 946. *Map 4, F7, p255* Comprehensive collection of flamenco performance on CD, DVD, and video.

Sports

Tarifa Piratas, Calle Batalla del Salado, Urb El Recreo 3, Tarifa, **T** 956 681 353. *Map 5, A1, p256* A world-famous shop for all things windsurfing.

Kiteboarding Company, Calle Mar Menor s/n, Tarifa, **T** 956 680 940. *Map 5, p256 (off map)* A new shop for all your kitesurfing needs.

The Costa de la Luz is a fantastic destination for an active holiday, with watersports enthusiasts particularly well catered for. The action centres on Tarifa, whose miles of sandy beaches and healthy breezes make it one of the world's prime destinations for windsurfing and its recent, exhilirating spin-off, kitesurfing. There are also bags of spots to just jump on a board the old-fashioned way, as well as opportunities to go diving or horse riding.

More traditional Spanish activities can also be enjoyed. El Puerto de Santa María has one of the most important bullrings in Spain, and aficionados argue long and loud in the town's seafood bars over the merits of what they have seen. And while the big-league action is up the road in Sevilla and Málaga, the local football teams lack neither pride nor ambition.

Bullfighting

Bullfighting is the most controversial and Andalucían of activities. Each town normally only has a few a year, usually all during its main summer fiesta. If you know you'll hate it, don't go; if you're not sure, go to one – even if you oppose it on principle. Tickets are generally pretty easy to get (except for the big-name fights); just turn up at the *taquilla* at the bullring (*plaza de toros*) the previous day or a few hours before. All the pageantry doesn't come cheap, however; count on at least €25 a ticket at prestigious venues such as El Puerto de Santa María and for big-name *toreros*. Tickets in the sun (*sol*) are the cheapest, followed by *sol y sombra* and *sombra* (shade). Within the sections, ringside seats (*barreras*) are the most expensive. The website www.mundotoro.com (Spanish only) has a useful search engine for upcoming dates.

Cycling

The section between Matalascañas and Mazagón is actually a dedicated cycleway/footpath called the **Camino Verde**. See Bicycle hire, p200.

Climbing

Spain is not generally thought of as a mecca for climbing, or *escalada*, but it is, nevertheless, a popular sport. There is good climbing at Cerro San Bartolo near Bolonia, among other places. Unlike climbing routes in Britain, which are generally unassisted, climbs in Andalucía are sport climbs, that is they are 'equipped' already with bolts and rings.

Sociedad Excursionista de Málaga, Calle República Argentina 9, 29016, Málaga, **T** 952 650 258.

Tarifa Climbing, Tarifa, **T** 665 475 845. Rock-climbing in the Tarifa area with an experienced and calm instructor.

Diving

Tarifa is the place for diving excursions.

Club Scorpora, Avenida Fuerzas Armadas s/n, **T** 629 546 177.

Hotel Fuerte Conil, Conil, **T** 630 234 426. There is a dive school based at the hotel that runs PADI courses.

Club de Buceo Bahía, Avenida Andalucía 1, **T** 956 054 626, www.aventuramarina.org.

Tarifa Diving, Avenida de la Constitución 10, **T** 639 186 070.

Fishing

It is a common sight in Andalucía to see people sea fishing from beaches and rocks, but what is not generally known is that there are also good opportunities for freshwater fishing. The prime location is the **Bornos Reservoir**, near Arcos de la Frontera, which has enormous numbers of carp. It's all regulated, and you'll need a permit (*permiso de pesca*), obtainable from the local Ayuntamiento and valid for two weeks. You should bring your own tackle as it is almost impossible to hire equipment. Further information is available from tourist offices; the local fishing shop is, as always, the best spot to ask about what's biting where. The **Federación Española de Pesca** (Calle Navas de Tolosa 3, Madrid, **T** 915 328 353), is another good starting point for information.

Calipsopesca, **T** 605 906 951, www.calipsopesca.com. Based out of Barbate, this outfit runs deep-sea fishing excursions, including the chance to battle half-ton tuna between July and November.

Football

Football is religion in Spain, and while the area covered by this book currently doesn't have a *Primera Liga* team, the local sides of Cádiz and Jerez are both doing their utmost to change that for the 2005-06 season. Tickets for home games usually go on sale at the ground three or four days before the games, which are typically on Sunday at 1700.

Cádiz Club de Fútbol, Estadio Ramón de Carranza, Plaza Madrid s/n, **T** 956 070 165, www.cadizcf.com.

Xerez Club Deportivo, Estadio Chapín, Avenida del Polo s/n, **T** 956 316 080, www.xerezcd.com.

Horse riding

Tarifa's long sandy beaches and wooded dunes are perfect for a gallop. If it's a bet you're after, head to Sanlúcar in August (see p51). For riding excursions, operators include:

Centro Ecuestre La Vega, Carretera N340 Km 83. **T** 677 287 929. *Close to Tarifa.*

El Pasodoble, Sector 9, parcela 90, Matalascañas, **T** 959 448 241, 629 060 545. Riding trips on the beach and in the dunes.

Hotel Dos Mares, Carretera N340 Km 79.5, **T** 626 480 019. *On the highway north of Tarifa.*

Hurricane Hotel, Carretera N340 Km 78, **T** 956 689 092. *On the highway north of Tarifa.*

Los Alamos Equestrian Holidays, Apdo 56, Barbate, Cádiz, **T**+34 956 437 416 (Spain), **T**+44 1684 567 266 (UK), www.losalamosriding.co.uk. Five-day horse riding trips around the beaches and forests of the Costa de la Luz.

Kitesurfing

Kitesurfing is the big thing in Tarifa at the moment and there are several places to hire equipment or learn the basics of this spectacular sport, most of them along the main road, Avenida Batalla del Salado. Expect to pay €80-100 for a two-hour beginners' class; most people are confident enough to strike out on their own after some four to six hours' tuition. The best conditions depend on the wind, but are typically in the afternoon, meaning that, if you fancy a go, you can wait until that morning before asking the experts in the shops if they think it's a good day for it.

Art of Kiting, Calle Batalla del Salado 47, **T** 956 685 204, www.artofkiting.com. A two-day beginners' course costs €180.

Club Mistral, at the Hurricane Hotel (see Windsurfing, below).

Kite School, Calle Batalla del Salado 28, **T** 956 627 005, sharki@tarifakite.com. One-on-one classes €100 for two hours, or €80 each if there are two of you. Group classes also available.

Spin-Out, Carretera Cádiz-Málaga Km 75.5, north of Tarifa, **T** 956 236 352, www.tarifaspinout.com. They also run classes for kids. You can pick up second-hand equipment here.

Motor racing

Situated 10 km east of Jerez is its Circuito Permanente de Velocidad (www.circuitodejerez.com). This racing track has hosted the Spanish Formula One Grand Prix in the past, and is the established venue for the motorcycling Grand Prix, which normally takes place in early May, close to the time of the Jerez fiesta. Throughout the year there are other motor-racing events here at weekends.

Surfing

The coastline of Andalucía is a mixture of long, dune-backed, sandy beaches and rocky points. The region around **Cádiz** is dominated by massive tracts of beach break. This area picks up less swell than the south due to the blocking effect of Cabo São Vicente in Portugal. The rocky points around **Cabo de Trafalgar** and **Cabo García** can have some excellent point breaks in good swells and the southern stretch of beach towards **Tarifa** can have great waves set against the backdrop of Africa's Northern Rif mountains.

Many of the breaks are pretty relaxed although Cádiz and **Roche**, further south, can get very busy. One of the most popular surfing beaches is **El Palmar**, south of Conil de la Frontera. Other good breaks are around **Chipiona**, **Chiclana de la Frontera**, and **Barbate**.

El Palmar Surf School, Paseo Marítimo s/n, opposite Casa Juan, El Palmar, **T** 606 942 895, surfelpalmar@yahoo.es.

Windsurfing

Tarifa's two major winds, the easterly *levante* and the westerly *poniente*, create excellent windsurfing conditions along the beautiful Playa de los Lances, which stretches from town 11 km north. There are heaps of windsurfing schools that give lessons and hire equipment. Board rental will cost about €50-60 per day, a full day's lesson is upward of €100.

Art of Surfing, Calle Batalla del Salado s/n, **T** 956 680 860.

BIC Sport Center, at the Hotel Dos Mares, Carretera N340 Km 79.5, **T** 630 342 258.

Club Mistral, at the Hurricane Hotel, Carretera N340 Km 78, **T** 956 689 098.

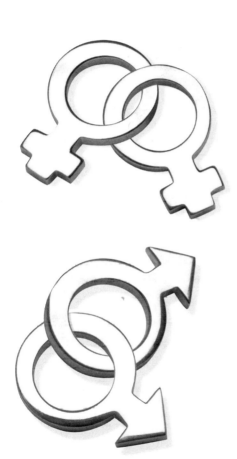

There are different levels of tolerance and open-mindedness towards gays and lesbians in Andalucía, but the Costa de la Luz is fairly accepting, particularly Cádiz, a city with a long tradition of open-mindedness. In summer resorts such as El Puerto de Santa María, the local gay and lesbian population is significantly boosted by tourists in the holiday season.

In other places, community attitudes are perhaps not quite 21st century in general, particularly among the older generations, but gay and lesbian visitors should encounter no problems at all, and will feel accepted in nearly all bars and nightclubs.

Venues are, however, very thin on the ground; the ones listed here are those that are predominantly gay and lesbian, but that's not to say that there's not plenty of folk that stay away from the scene; most of the *discotecas* of Jerez and Cádiz have at least an element at weekends.

Bars and clubs

Café de Aquitania, Calle Luna 7, El Puerto de Santa María,
T 656 485 308. *Mon-Wed 0830-2300, Thu-Sat 0830-late*.
Map 2, D5, p252 A sleek and friendly bar decorated in pastel
shades and black and white photos. It's a relaxed spot for a coffee
or a drink; be sure to check out the cute and colourful toilets.
Mixed crowd in the evenings.

Café Poniente, Calle Beato Diego de Cádiz 18, Cádiz, **T** 956 212
697. *Daily 2230-0430. Map 1, B7, p251* The old reliable standby of
the Cádiz scene, this friendly café is a good spot to start out your
night and has a mostly gay male clientele. There are often drag
shows on stage.

Dock, Calle Bolos 4, El Puerto de Santa María. *Map 2, G3,
p252* Fairly sedate off-season, this *discoteca* revs up during the
summer months.

Duplicado, Plaza Vargas 2, Jerez de la Frontera, **T** 956 326 329.
Map 4, F5, p254 A beautifully decorated bar, attractively done
out in wood and brick with hanging musical instruments.
There's a friendly bohemian clientele, with a strong gay and
lesbian element.

El Burladero, Carretera Faro de Trafalgar s/n. *Map 6, G4,
p257* On the way to the Trafalgar lighthouse, this is the most
gay-friendly of the summer *discotecas* of Los Caños de Meca, which
is a popular destination.

Fangoria's, Guadalcacín, Jerez de la Frontera. *Map 6, D4, p257*
In a small village 2 km east of Jerez, this is the best option in the area.
It's a popular gay and lesbian *discoteca* with a terrace for outdoor

revelry on summer nights. Open Thursday and Friday nights only, the emphasis is on fun, with such shenanigans as wet T-shirt contests. Get a cab here if you're going to drink; police checks are common.

Gladiator, Paseo Marítimo s/n, Cádiz, near the corner of Calle Sirena. *Map 1, F12, p251 (off map)* Spacious bar mainly frequented by gay men. In summer, there's a great outdoor terrace looking over the sand and sea.

La Gorda te da de Comer, Calle General Luque 1, Cádiz. *Map 1, B7, p251* See p124. As well as being one of the city's best tapas bars, this is a good spot to meet people before heading down the road to La Luna or Poniente.

La Luna, Calle Doctor Zurita s/n, Cádiz. *1200-0500 or later Tue-Sun. Map 1, B7, p251* This bar in the old town of Cádiz is a long-time favourite among the nightspots of the area, and together with the Poniente, forms as much of a pink zone as can be found in these parts. It's still the place to go for lesbians, who form the vast majority of the clientele. Starts quiet and ends up wild.

Pasaje, Calle Pedro Cortés 6, Tarifa. *Map 5, D4, p256* A cool discobar featuring DJs pumping out the house music and a trendily dressed crowd with a high gay presence.

Pub Averno, Calle San Antonio Abad 5, Cádiz, **T** 956 265 013. *Map 1, E9, p251* This characterful spot tucked away in the Barrio del Pópulo is one of the city's best gay bars. There are regular drag and strip shows and a warm atmosphere, with folk dancing happily until very late at night.

Too Much, Plaza Elías Auja s/n, El Puerto de Santa María.
Map 2, H1, p252 Right by the bullring, this friendly spot starts off
the evening doing tapas, with a quiet atmosphere perfect for a
chat; later on the sounds crank up and the lights dim down and it
becomes a disco-bar.

Shops

Arsénico, Calle Valverde 3, Cádiz, **T** 956 228 122.
Map 1, C7, p251 Gay and lesbian-friendly shop selling clothing
and accessories.
Internacional, Calle Murillo 2, Cádiz, **T** 956 262 000.
Daily 1000-2200. Map 1, F12, p251 (off map) Popular sex shop.

Saunas

Termas Gades, Calle General Muñoz Arenillas 9, Cádiz.
Map 1, F12, p251 (off map) Popular gay sauna with good facilities
and atmosphere.

Organizations

Arcadia, Calle Cervantes 19, Cádiz, **T** 956 212 200. *1900-2200.*
Map 1, C5, p250 Affable and diverse queer collective.

Colega Andaluza, Calle Encarnación 5, Cádiz, **T** 956 226 262.
Map 1, E4, p250 Cádiz branch of a nationwide gay and
lesbian association.

Cogailes, www.cogailes.org, **T** 900 601 601 (freephone hotline
1800-2200 daily), is a gay and lesbian organization with a handy
information service.

Girasol, **T** 958 200 602. An Andalucía-wide lesbian and gay association based in Granada.

Jerelesgay, **T** 696 917 832, http://jerelesgay.patalata.net
An association of gays and lesbians in Jerez de la Frontera.

Magazines and newspapers

Shanguide is a useful magazine, with reviews, events, information and city-by-city listings for the whole country.

Websites

www.gayinspain.com/andalucia/cadiz.htm.
Listings of bars, clubs, zones, etc.

www.solodecontactos.com.
Gay contacts by Spanish province.

www.colegaweb.net.
The website of a national gay and lesbian association.

www.es.gay.com.
National portal of principal use for contacts and chat.

www.damron.com.
Although most of the listings are only available via subscription, this online database of venues and travel information is worthwhile.

Spain is an excellent place to travel with children, and no region more so than the Costa de la Luz, where yawn-inducing visits to archaeological museums can be skilfully balanced with sessions on the kilometres of sandy beaches hereabouts. And when the sandcastles lose their appeal, there are plenty of alternative entertainments; the region is popular with holidaying Spanish families too.

Kids are kings in Spain and it's one of the easiest places to take them along on holiday. Children socialize with their parents from an early age here and you'll see them eating in restaurants and out in bars well after midnight. The outdoor summer life and high pedestrianization of the cities is especially suitable and stress free for both you and the kids to enjoy the experience.

Few places, however, are equipped with high-chairs, unbreakable plates or baby-changing facilities. Children are basically expected to eat the same sort of things as their parents, although you'll sometimes see a *menú infantil* at a restaurant, which typically has simpler dishes and smaller portions than the norm.

The cut-off age for children paying half or no admission/passage on public transport and in tourist attractions varies widely. RENFE trains let under-fours on free, and its discount passage of around 50% is until 12.

Most car-rental companies have child seats available, but it's wise to book these in advance, particularly in summer.

Activities and tours

Cádiz to El Puerto de Santa María *El Vaporcito, Map 1, D6, p250 See also p27.* The boat ride across the bay takes 40 minutes and is a great trip.

Football, p183 Despite recent press, the atmosphere at Spanish football games is generally happy and very unintimidating; a lot of families and children are present, and there's no alcohol consumed.

Girasol, Calle Colón 12, Tarifa, **T**652 868 929, www.girasol-adventure.com *Map 5, D3, p256* Tarifa-based set-up running excursions in the region. They have a special one-day climbing course for kids (2 hours, €24), and they also run tennis courses for children.

Horse carriages *Map 2, D6, p252* Take a ride around town in a horse carriage. The most popular place to do it is from the Plaza de las Galeras in El Puerto de Santa María (summer only). Haggle for a good price.

Kitesurfing *See also p184* Most of the companies based in Tarifa will happily accept kids for lessons in this exciting sport. It is recommended as suitable for eight year-olds and above.

Kids

Turmares Tarifa, Puerto de Tarifa s/n, Tarifa, **T** 956 680 741. *Map 5, G4, p256* Afternoon trips out of Tarifa in the summer, with an almost guaranteed chance of seeing dolphins, and the possibility of whales and orcas. The trips are family-friendly and take two and a half hours.

Attractions and museums

Aqualand, Carretera El Puerto-Jerez, **T** 956 870 511, www.aqualand.es. *Exit 646 on the N-IV. Mid Jun-early Sep 1100-1800 (1900 in Jul and Aug), 3-12 year olds €11, adults €15.50. Map 6, D4, p257* This popular summer waterpark is a huge complex of pools and waterslides, which include the giant Crazy Race, and the scarier Black Hole. It's a fine spot for a relaxed day out; the only drawback can be the queues for the in-demand attractions. If you don't have transport, you can get there on bus No 26 from El Puerto de Santa María, which runs about every 40 minutes.

Conil de la Frontera *Map 6, F4, p257 See also p154* A calm and shallow town beach, one of the area's best for kids.

González Byass *Map 4, H3, p254 See also p76* If you want to visit a sherry bodega, this is the most child-friendly tour, with its cute train and drinking mice.

Museo de la Miel y las Abejas, Carretera Cortes-Cuartillo Km 2, **T** 956 237 528. *13 km southeast of Jerez (head for Cortes). Map 6, E4, p257* This cheery ranch produces well-regarded honey and has recently set up a museum explaining the process. You can watch the bees going about their business in an open hive, and there's plenty of open space as well as a playground.

Museo del Mundo Marino, Parque Dunar s/n, Matalascañas. **T** 959 506 129, *Tue-Sat 1000-1400, 1530-1800, Sun 1000-1400, €5. Map 6, B2, p257* A modern and interesting display covering all aspects of dune and maritime ecology, particularly focusing on the Bahía de Cádiz area. Some impressive whale skeletons and models are among the favourites, but it's not an aquarium; there are no fishtanks.

Real Escuela Andaluza de Arte Ecuestre, *Map 4, A6, p254 See also p75* Although younger children might get bored, older ones will appreciate the horseplay.

Torre de Tavira, Cádiz, *Map 1, D6, p251 See also p43* The camera obscura is fascinating, as is the one in the Alcázar in Jerez, *Map 4, H4, p254 See also p69.*

Zoo Botánico, Calle Taxdirt s/n, Jerez de la Frontera, **T** 956 182 397, www.zoobotanicojerez.com. *Mid-Jun to mid-Sep daily 1000-2000, mid-Sep to mid-Jun Tue-Sun 1000-1800, €2.70 for 3-13 year olds, €4.20 for 14 and above. Map 4, A1, p254 (off map)* One of Spain's best zoos, this large leafy complex has all your favourite animals: kangaroos, hippos, chimps, elephants and even a rare white tiger.

Shops

Goya, Calle Columela 22, Cádiz, **T** 956 222 282. *Map 1, C7, p251* Good-looking Spanish fashion for kids.

Heladería Bornay, Sanlúcar de Barrameda. *Map 3, F4, p253 See also p130* Nowhere better than here for an ice cream, where they do them best.

Imaginarium, Calle Ancha 4, Cádiz, **T** 956 223 953. *Map 1, B5, p250* A branch of a successful and innovative Spanish toy chain. There's even a separate kids' entrance!

Sleeping

El Palomar de la Breña T 956 435 003, www.palomardelabrena.com. *Located 6 km from Los Caños de Meca See also p111*. This is an excellent place to stay with small children. It's a long way from any roads and has big grounds to wander; it's a short drive to the beach, and the hotel offers a childminding service if you fancy a bit of time off.

Hurricane Hotel, Carretera N340, Km 78, **T** 956 684 919, www.hotelhurricane.com. *6 km north of Tarifa See also p184*. Right on the beach, this is a family-friendly hotel with childminding facilities.

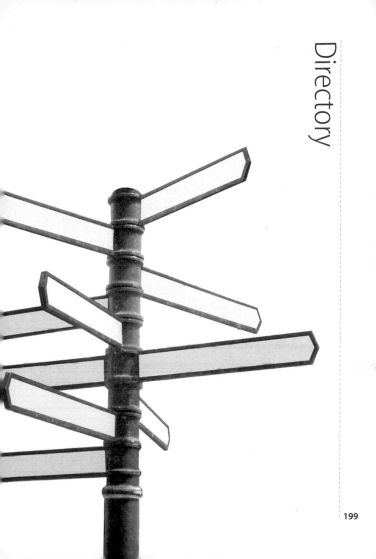

Directory

Airline offices
Air Berlin, Aeropuerto de Jerez, **T** 956 150 120, www.airberlin.com; **Iberia**, Aeropuerto de Jerez, **T** 956 150 009, www.iberia.com; **Ryanair**, Aeropuerto de Jerez, **T** 956 150 152, www.ryanair.com.

Banks and ATMs
There are banks all over the place, all with ATMs that accept Cirrus, Maestro, Visa, MasterCard, and most other international credit and debit cards. This is by far the best way of managing money. If you need an exchange, banking hours are Mon-Fri 0900-1400 and Sat 0900-1300 (only in winter months). Outside these hours, you can change money at major hotels or El Corte Inglés department store at murderous rates.

Bicycle hire
Bicicletas Bigote, Edificio Oasis, Av Rodrigo de Bastida, El Puerto de Santa María, **T** 956 875 418, Mon-Fri 1000-1400, 1730-2030, Sat 1000-1400.
Conil Rent, C Gonzalo Sánchez Fuentes 14, Conil de la Frontera, **T** 956 441 536, www.conil-rent.de. Rent a good range of bicycles and motorbikes on a daily or weekly basis.

Car hire
Bahía, Plaza de Sevilla s/n, Cádiz, **T** 956 271 895.
Hertz (www.hertz.com, **T** 902 402 405, Jerez Airport, Sevilla Airport, Málaga Airport, Cádiz).
Atesa (www.atesa.es): Jerez Airport (**T** 956 150 014), Sevilla Airport, Cádiz (**T** 956 266 645), Jerez (**T** 956 313 206), Málaga Airport (**T** 952 048 503).
Easycar (www.easycar.com, Jerez Airport, Jerez, Sevilla, Cádiz, Málaga Airport).
Star Rent a Car (www.rentspain.com, Jerez Airport, Málaga Airport).

Consulates
Australia, C Federico Rubio 14, Sevilla **T** 954 220 971.
Britain, Av Ramón de Carranza 26-27, Cádiz, **T** 956 286 700.
France, Plaza Santa Cruz 1, Sevilla, **T** 954 222 896. **Germany**,
Av Palmera 19, Sevilla, **T** 954 230 204. **Morocco**, Con
Descubrimientos s/n, Sevilla, **T** 954 081 044. **Netherlands**, Av
Ramón de Carranza 26-27, Cádiz, **T** 954 280 866. **USA**, Paseo
Delicias 7, Sevilla, **T** 954 231 885.

Credit card lines
Amex, **T** 902 375 637; **Mastercard**, **T** 900 971 231;
Visa, **T** 900 951 125

Dentists
There are numerous dentists in Cádiz and Jerez; the tourist office
can help locate one nearby. For dental emergencies there's a
rotating roster of dentists, so call in the first instance **T** 902 505
061, the general number for health emergencies in Andalucía.

Disabled travel
Spain isn't the best equipped of countries in terms of disabled
travel, but things are improving rapidly. By law, all new public
buildings have to have full disabled access and facilities, but
disabled toilets are rare in other edifices. Facilities generally are
significantly better in Andalucía than in the rest of the country.
Most trains and stations are wheelchair friendly to some degree, as
are many urban buses, but intercity buses are largely inaccessible
for wheelies. Hertz in Málaga and Sevilla have a small range of cars
set up for disabled drivers, but be sure to book them well in
advance. Nearly all underground and municipal car parks have lifts
and disabled spaces, as do many museums, castles, etc.

The regional accommodation lists, available from tourist offices,
are an invaluable resource for finding a bed. Most include a
disabled-access criterion. Many *pensiones* are in buildings with

ramps and lifts, but there are many that are not, and the lifts can be very small. Nearly all *paradores* and modern chain hotels are fully wheelchair accessible, but it's best to phone. Be sure to confirm details as many hotels' claims are well intentioned but not fully thought through.

Useful organizations
Confederación Nacional de Sordos de España (CNSE), www.cnse.es, has links to local associations for the deaf.
Federación ECOM, **T**+34 934 515 550, www.ecom.es, is a helpful Barcelona-based organization for the disabled that can assist in providing information on disabled-friendly tourist facilities throughout the country.
Global Access, www.geocities.com/Paris/1502/index.html, has regular reports from disabled travellers as well as links to other sites.
Mobility Abroad, **T**+44 1375 377 246 (UK) or **T**+34 952 447 764 (Spain), www.mobilityabroad.com, is a Málaga-based organization that provides support and hire of wheelchairs and disabled vehicles.
RADAR, **T**+44 20 7250 3222, www.radar.org.uk, is a British network for the disabled that can help members get information and contacts for disabled travel around Europe.

Doctors
For an emergency, see **Emergency numbers** and **Hospitals** below. For a non-emergency, ask for a **Centro de Salud**: **Cádiz** C Cervantes 9, **T** 956 225 469; **Jerez** C José Luis Díez 14, **T** 956 033 665. In all cases you'll need a copy of the new Form E111 or, soon, the European Health Insurance Card (EU residents; available from post offices in Britain), or proof of coverage if you don't want to pay.

Electricity
Spain runs on 220V, as does most of Europe, with a two-pin plug.

Emergency numbers
For general emergencies, call **T** 112. For the police, call **T** 091 (092 for the local police, who deal in everyday matters), for an ambulance **T** 061. There's a line for reporting crimes on **T** 902 102 112.

Hospitals
Cádiz: Hospital Universitario, Av Ana de Viya 21, **T** 956 002 100.
Jerez: Hospital General, Ctra de Circunvalación s/n, **T** 956 032 000.

Internet/email
Connection is normally pretty good and access usually costs €1-3 per hour. Many cybercafés are open well into the wee hours, although you'll have to cope with the shellbursts and automatic weaponfire from online games, which are also very popular. Most modern hotels above a certain standard have walljacks where you can connect a laptop.

Cádiz
San Rafael, C Benjumeda 38, Mon-Fri 1000-1400, 1700-2200, Sat 1000-1500, €2 per hr; **Enreda 2**, C Cervantes 18, €1.50 per hr, daily 1100-1500, 1600-2200, on the corner of C San José; **Ciber Papelería**, C Aduana 13, near tourist office; **Red**, Cuesta de las Calesas 43, reasonable internet access at €1.80 per hr, cheaper between 1500 and 1700. Also a *locutorio* for making telephone calls; **Novap**, next door, is similar.

El Puerto de Santa María
Rush@Net, C Virgen de los Milagros 137; **CiberBahía**, C Micaela Aramburu 21.

Sanlúcar de Barrameda
Cyber Guadalquivir, C Infanta Beatriz 8, has a good connection and computers named after world cities, €1.80 per hr.

Jerez de la Frontera
Internet Centernet, Av Arcos 1, charges €1.80 per hr for a good internet connection; **San Pedro**, C Bizcocheros 2, is a handy central bar with decent internet access.

Conil
Café de la Habana, Pl Santa Catalina s/n, **T** 956 443 484, daily 1030-0130. Access at €3 per hr.

Barbate
CB System, C Calvo Sotelo 8, **T** 956 430 803. €2 per hr.

Tarifa
Pandora, C Sancho IV El Bravo 3, reasonable connection, €3 per hr; **Navegante**, C General Copons 1, €3 per hr; **Planet**, Plaza del Angel s/n, €3 per hr; **CyberTarifa**, C María Antonia Toldeo 3, €1.80 per hr.

Vejer de la Frontera
Cyber Sancho IV, Arco del Mayorazgo s/n, is a handy cybercafé around the corner from the Plaza de España opposite the Mayorazgo building.

Mazagón
Locutorio, Av Fuentepiña 3. Internet access on the main pedestrian street for €2 per hr.

Language schools
Colegio de Español la Janda, C José Castrillón 22, Vejer de la Frontera, **T** 956 447 060, www.lajanda.org.

Escuela Hispalense, Av Fuerzas Armadas 1, Tarifa, **T** 956 680 927, www.hispalense.com.
Linguae Mundi, C Enrique Rivero 18, Jerez de la Frontera, **T** 956 349 696, www.linguae-mundi.com.
SIC, C Condesa Villafuente Bermeja 7, Cádiz, **T** 956 252 724, www.spanishincadiz.com.

Launderette
Acuario, C Colón 12, Tarifa, **T** 956 627 037.

Left luggage
There are left luggage facilities at the railway stations in Cádiz and Jerez de la Frontera.

Motorcycle hire
Conil Rent, C Gonzalo Sánchez Fuentes 14, Conil de la Frontera, **T** 956 441 536, www.conil-rent.de. A good range of bicycles and motorbikes for rent on a daily or weekly basis.

Media
The national dailies, **El País**, **El Mundo** and the rightist **ABC**, are read, but local papers attract a high readership. These are the **Diario de Cádiz** and **Diario de Jerez**, as well as the Algeciras-based **El Faro Información**, which covers the southern part of the coast. The sports dailies **Marca** and **As**, dedicated mostly to football, have a massive readership that rivals any of the broadsheets (Marca has the highest circulation of any Spanish daily). There's no tabloid press as such; the closest equivalent is the *prensa de corazón* and the gossip magazines such as **¡Hola!**, forerunner of Britain's Hello! English-language newspapers are widely available in kiosks in the larger towns.

Opticians
Multiópticas, Calle Larga 31, Jerez de la Frontera, **T** 956 344 422.
Ulloa Optico, Calle Ancha 21, Cádiz, **T** 956 224 205.

Pharmacies (late night)
Pharmacies are everywhere, and the staff highly qualified. They take it in turns to open at weekends and at night. Every pharmacy has the current roster posted in the window (*farmacías de guardia*), as do the local newspapers.

Police
Dial **T** 091 for a police emergency, **T** 092 to speak to the local police.

Post offices
Mon-Fri 0830-2030, Sat 0930-1400. Stamps (*sellos*) can be bought only at post offices or tobacconists (*estancos*). A letter to the rest of the EU costs €0.51. **Cádiz**: Plaza Topete s/n, Cádiz, **T** 956 210 511. **Jerez**: C Cerrón 2, **T** 956 342 295.

Public holidays
For local holidays, see Festivals, p165.
1 Jan, Año Nuevo (New Year's Day); **6 Jan**, Reyes Magos/Epifanía (Epiphany), when Christmas presents are given; **Easter**, Jueves Santo, Viernes Santo, Día de Pascua (Maundy Thursday, Good Friday, Easter Sunday); **28 Feb**, Día de Andalucía (Andalucía Day); **1 May**, Fiesta de Trabajo (Labour Day); **15 Aug**, Asunción (Feast of the Assumption); **12 Oct**, Día de la Hispanidad (Spanish National Day, Columbus Day, Feast of the Virgin of the Pillar); **1 Nov**, Todos los Santos (All Saints' Day); **6 Dec**, Día de la Constitución Española (Constitution Day); **8 Dec**, Inmaculada Concepción (Feast of the Immaculate Conception); **25 Dec**, Navidad (Christmas Day).

Taxi firms
Cádiz, T 956 212 121; **Conil**, T 956 440 787; **Jerez**, T 956 344 860; **Los Caños de Meca**, T 619 879 571; **Tarifa**, T 956 684 421.

Telephone
The international dialling code for Spain is +34. To make an international call from Spain, dial 00 followed by the country code. Calls within Spain begin with a three-digit area code (eg Cádiz province is 956); this must be dialled in all cases. Mobile numbers begin with 6. Public phones accept coins and cards, and all have international direct dialling, although you'll save money by buying a prepaid card (*tarjeta telefónica prepagada*) from a kiosk. Cheap phone calls can also be made from *locutorios* (call centres).

Most foreign mobiles will work in Spain (although most North American ones won't); check with your service provider about what the call costs will be like. Many mobile networks require you to call up before leaving your home country to activate overseas service. Spanish recharge cards for multinational companies, such as Vodafone, will work on foreign mobiles. If you're staying a while, it may be cheaper to buy a Spanish mobile, as there are always numerous offers and discounts.

Time
Spain is one hour ahead of GMT, and puts its clocks forward and back at the same time as Britain and the rest of Europe.

Toilets
Public toilets are few, but most bars won't have a problem with you using theirs, as long as you ask. Be warned: few have locks or paper. *Caballeros* (occasionally *Señores*) is blokes, and *Señoras* is girls. Toilets are indicated by any of the following: *Aseos*, *Baños*, *Servicios*, or *HHSS*.

Transport enquiries
Cádiz bus station, **T** 956 211 763; **Jerez Airport**, **T** 956 150 000;
Jerez bus station, **T** 956 342 174; **Trains**, RENFE, **T** 902 240 202.

Travel agents
Viajes Marsans, Avenida Ramón de Carranza 22, Cádiz, **T** 956 284
711, www.marsans.es. **Halcón Viajes**, Calle Drago 1, Cádiz, **T** 956
263 559, www.halconviajes.com. **Viajes Sherry Tours**, Calle
Larga 23, Jerez de la Frontera, **T** 956 343 912. **Viajes Zafiro**, Calle
Beato Juan Grande 9, Jerez de la Frontera, **T** 956 350 018.

A sprint through history

Mists of time
Ancestors of modern humans move into the peninsula from Africa, presumably entering Europe via the Costa de la Luz area more than 500,000 years ago. A 60,000-year-old fossilized female cranium found in nearby Gibraltar is the first evidence of Neanderthal man ever brought to light.

6000-3000 BC
Neolithic period; the first settlements in the area appear, along with evidence of agriculture, domestication and ceramic production.

3000-1100 BC
Chalcolithic period and Bronze Age, with working of copper, followed by alloys. The Guadalquivir valley is probably only used seasonally due to flooding.

1100-1000 BC
Iberians, probably of local origin, inhabit the area, and are joined by some Celts and the Phoenicians; the latter set up trading stations on the Andalucían coast, including Cádiz, which they name Gadir; inhabitants of today's Cádiz are still called *gaditanos*.

500-206 BC
As Phoenician power wanes the Carthaginians, settle widely in Andalucía, particularly Cádiz. They take control of much of southern Spain. Some towns accept Carthaginian control while others resist it.

206 BC
Roman troops arrive in Spain in 218 BC and Andalucía becomes one of the major theatres of the Second Punic War. The final Roman victory over the Carthaginians comes in 206 BC, at the Battle of Ilipa near Sevilla.

206 BC–AD 426	The Romans set about conquering the whole of Hispania. They are the first to create the idea of Spain as a single geographical entity, a concept it has been struggling with ever since. Roman customs rub off on the Iberians; local languages gradually disappear as Latin becomes predominant. A gradual decline begins in the late 2nd century AD; by the fourth century, things are really on the slide and Cádiz is virtually in ruins.
711	The Islamic invasion. After a number of exploratory raids, the Moors defeat and slay the Visigothic king Roderic somewhere near Tarifa. In less than three years almost the whole peninsula is in Moorish hands; an extraordinary feat.
756	The Córdoba caliphate is declared, and the flowering of Moorish Spain commences. Meanwhile, the Asturian kingdom in the north begins to grow in strength and the long process of the Christian 'Reconquista' (Reconquest) begins.
13th century	Jerez, named Sherish by the Moors, is conquered in 1251 by the Christian king Fernando III, but is subsequently lost in 1264; the commander of the Christian garrison, García Gómez Carillo, promptly assembles a force and retakes the city, this time permanently. The borders of Moorish Granada lay just to the east, earning Jerez and other towns the surname 'de la Frontera' (of the frontier).

1492	The Catholic Monarchs, Fernando and Isabel, conquer the last Moorish bastion, Granada, and expel Spain's Jewish population. Columbus discovers America. Under their patronage he sails from Palos de la Frontera with a crew drawn from the area. This marks the beginning of Andalucía's golden age of trade and wealth.
1519	Magellan sets sail from Sanlúcar de Barrameda attempting a circumnavigation of the world. He doesn't make it, but one of his ships, skippered by Juan Sebastián Elkano, does, arriving three years later.
1587	Sir Francis Drake, under orders from Queen Elizabeth, attacks a Spanish fleet anchored in Cádiz and ransacks part of the town in an operation famously described as having "singed the King of Spain's beard".
Early 18th century	Ailing, heirless Charles II dies, naming the French duke Philip of Bourbon as his successor, much to the concern of England and Holland, who declare war on France. The conflict is eventually resolved at the Treaty of Utrecht when Britain receives Gibraltar, and Spain also loses its Italian and Low Country possessions.
1717	New World trade is officially transferred from Sevilla to Cádiz, an enormous boost for the city which now attracts the attention of foreign powers, who regularly came to loot the town.

1805	A turbulent century kicks off with a heavy defeat for a Spanish-French navy by Nelson off Cabo Trafalgar.
1812-1823	Liberal Cortes (assembly) in Cádiz draw up a constitution establishing a democratic parliamentary monarchy of sorts. The king, Fernando, revokes it and the Cortes eventually surrender in September 1823.
1835	Church and monastery property is confiscated in the Disentailment Act. The sale of the vast estates aids nobody but the large landowners, who buy them up at bargain prices, further skewing the distribution of arable land in Andalucía towards the wealthy.
Early 20th century	The growing disaffection of Andalucían farmworkers, forced for centuries into seasonal labour on the vast *latifundias*, leads to a strong anarchist movement in the region.
1923-1931	General Miguel Primo de Rivera, a native of Jerez de la Frontera, leads a coup and installs himself as dictator under King Alfonso. Alfonso is soon toppled as republicanism sweeps the country. The anti-royalists achieve excellent results in local elections in 1931 and the king is exiled. The ill-fated Second Republic is joyfully proclaimed by the left.
1936-1939	The Spanish Civil War; Cádiz is on the side of the left but can't hold out long against the Nationalists. Franco advances through Andalucía; his battle-hardened troops meet with little resistance.

1939-1975 The Franco years. Franco bans Cádiz's Carnaval during his rule (it survives by changing name and date). In the 1950s, Eisenhower recognizes the dictatorship as legitimate in exchange for Spanish support against the Eastern Bloc. American airbases are established in Spain; one of the biggest at Rota, near Chipiona.

1980s In 1982, the Socialist government (PSOE) of *sevillano* Felipe González is elected. The *comunidades autónomas* are created, and the regions of Spain are given their own parliaments. The Socialists oversee Spain's entry into the EEC (now EU) in 1986.

1996 The rightist Partido Popular forms a government under José María Aznar López. Economically conservative, Aznar uses the prevailing international climate to take strong action against ETA. His heavy-handed and undemocratic methods appall international observers and stirs the ghosts of Francoism in Spain. He takes the country to war in Iraq against the wishes of a majority of the population.

2004 11 March, three days before the general election, 10 bombs explode in Madrid; over 200 people are killed. The government blames ETA, despite substantial evidence for involvement by Islamic extremists. The electorate is outraged at what is perceived as a vote-minded cover-up and the PSOE are elected to government. The new prime minister, José Luis Rodrí-guez Zapatero, pledges to withdraw Spanish troops from Iraq and re-align the country with 'old Europe'.

Art and architecture

1st millennium BC

Iberian cultures produce fine jewellery from gold and silver, as well as some remarkable sculpture and ceramics. These influences derive from contact with trading posts set up by the Phoenicians, who have also left artistic evidence of their presence, some of which can be seen in the Museo de Cádiz.

The Carthaginians', on the other hand, have left little in the archaeological record; their principal base in Andalucía was Cádiz, but two millennia of subsequent occupation have taken their toll.

206 BC-AD 426

Roman Period The Romans bring their own artistic styles to the peninsula; there are many cultural remnants, including some fine sculpture and a number of elaborate mosaïc floors. Baelo Claudia, near Tarifa, is an impressive, if not especially well-preserved Roman town, and Cádiz preserves some remains, notably a recently excavated theatre.

426-711

Visigothic Period The Visigoths were skilled artists and craftspeople, and produced many fine pieces, notably in metalwork, but little remains from this period in the Costa de la Luz region.

711-1022

Ummayad Period The majority of the artistic heritage left by the Moors is tied up in their architecture. They introduce compact, climate-driven urban planning to Andalucía, still very visible in towns like Vejer de la Frontera and Tarifa. Tarifa's castle was built in the 10th century to combat pirates in the Straits of Gibraltar.

1147-mid 13th century	**Almohad Period** Much of the region's Moorish architectural heritage dates from this period. The Almohads fortified their towns, building simple, attractive, and effective walls and towers, including that of the Alcázar de Jerez. *Azulejos*, the colourful painted tiles so typical of southern Spain, were first used during this period, as was the ornamental brickwork that also characterized later *mudéjar* architecture. Fabulous inlaid wooden ceilings were another innovation that was continued and developed for many more centuries.
Mid 13th-early 16th century	**Gothic-Mudéjar Period** As the Christians took Andalucía back piece by piece, they introduced their own styles, developed in the north with substantial influence from France and Italy. The Romanesque barely features in Andalucía; it was the Gothic style that influenced post-Reconquista church building in the 13th, 14th and 15th centuries. It was combined with styles learned under the Moors to form an Andalucían fusion known as Gothic-Mudéjar. Many of the region's churches are constructed on these lines, typically featuring a rectangular floor plan with a triple nave surrounded by pillars, a polygonal chancel and square chapels. The tower of Jerez's cathedral is a fine example of the *mudéjar* style, while Nuestra Señora de los Milagros in El Puerto de Santa María is classic Andalucían Gothic.

16th and 17th centuries	**The Renaissance** Nearby Sevilla was one of the centres of the Spanish Renaissance, and wealth seemed limitless. A fabulous series of paintings by one of the greatest artists of the period, Zurbarán, was produced for the Carthusian monastery at Jerez, and now can be seen in the Museo de Cádiz.
Fine 16th-century *palacios* can be found in nearly every town and city in the area (except Cádiz); these noble buildings were the homes of the aristocrats who had reaped the riches of the Reconquista and the new trade routes to the Americas.
17th and 18th centuries	**The Baroque** This was a time of great genius in architecture as in the other arts in Spain, as masters playfully explored the reaches of their imaginations. Churches became ever larger – in part to justify the huge façades – and nobles indulged in one-upmanship, building ever-grander *palacios*. The façades themselves are typified by such features as pilasters (narrow piers descending to a point) and niches to hold statues. Cádiz cathedral is largely built in this style.
18th and 19th centuries	**Neoclassical** This was an inevitable reaction to such *joie-de-vivre*. It again resorted to the cleaner lines of antiquity, which were used this time for public spaces as well as civic and religious buildings. Many plazas and town halls are in this style in places such as Cádiz, whose elegant old town is largely in this style.

Late 19th-early 20th century

Awakened interest in the days of Al-Andalus led to the neo-*mudéjar* (neo-Moorish) style being used for public buildings and private residences, such as the ornate fantasies as the Palacio de Orléans-Borbon in Sanlúcar de Barrameda, or the Gran Teatro Falla in Cádiz.

20th century

Elegance and whimsy never seemed to play much part in fascist architecture, and during the Franco era Andalucía was subjected to an appalling series of ponderous concrete monoliths, all in the name of progress. A few avant-garde buildings managed to escape the drudgery from the 1950s on, but it was the dictator's death in 1975 followed by EEC membership in 1986 that really provided the impetus for change.

A couple of painters stand out: sober 20th-century painter Daniel Vásquez Díaz, a Huelvan who adorned the walls of La Rábida monastery with murals on the life of Columbus; and, more recently, the contemporary artist and painter Guillermo Pérez Villalta, born in Tarifa, who has achieved much recognition.

Flamenco

Like bullfighting, flamenco as we know it is a fairly young art, having basically developed in the 19th century. It is constantly evolving, and there have been significant changes in its performance in the last century, which makes the search for 'classic' flamenco something of a wild goose chase. Rather, the thing to search for is authentic emotion and, beyond this, *duende*, an undefinable passion that carries singer and watchers away in a whirlwind of raw feeling, with a devil-may-care sneer at destiny.

Though there have been many excellent *payo* flamenco artists, its history is primarily a gypsy one. It was developed among gitanos in the Sevilla/Cádiz area but clearly includes elements of cultures encountered further away. Watching flamenco is like browsing through a travelogue; one moment you seem to be in Arabia, other moments recall Greece, southern India, Georgia, Israel. Flamenco sometimes feels primal and ancient, but that perhaps is also a function of it being so very different from most European musical tradition.

For a foreigner, perhaps the classic image of flamenco is a woman in a theatrical dress clicking castanets. A more authentic image is of a singer and guitarist, both sitting rather disconsolately on ramshackle chairs, or perhaps on a wooden box to tap out a rhythm. The singer and the guitarist work together, sensing the mood of the other and improvising. A beat is provided by clapping of hands or tapping of feet (don't join in!). If there's a dancer, he or she will lock into the mood of the others and vice-versa. The dancing is stop-start, frenetic, reminiscent (in spirit only) of what Zorba the Greek was getting at. Castanets are an optional accessory. The flamenco can reach crescendoes of frightening intensity when it seems the singer will have a stroke, the dancer is about to murder someone and the guitarist may never find it back to the world of the sane.

These outbursts of passion are seen to their fullest in *cante jondo*, the deepest and saddest form of flamenco, songs about the tragedies of life, love, and death. Lighter in mood is *cante chico*, which has a closer relation to Andalucían folk music. Related to flamenco, but not 'pure', are *sevillanas*, danced till you drop at Jerez's *feria*, and *rocieras*, which are sung on (and about) the annual *romería* pilgrimage to El Rocío.

Flamenco has waxed and waned in popularity over the years but is currently in a boom, partly due to the numbers of tourists who are interested in seeing it. One figure who played a great part in its revival was El Camarón de la Isla. From San Fernando just south of Cádiz, this gypsy singer, a gaunt, heroin-addicted genius, seemed to embody the romance, the passion and the dark side of the art.

Books

The Costa de la Luz is famous for producing two of the 20th century's most influential literary figures: Juan Ramón Jiménez and Rafael Alberti.

A member of the so-called Generation of 1898, a movement of writers and painters seeking to bring Spain forward into the postcolonial era, **Juan Ramón Jiménez** (1881-1958) hailed from Moguer in Huelva province and won the Nobel Prize for literature in 1956. His finest work is the long prose poem *Platero y yo*, a lyrical portrait of the town and the region conducted as a conversation between the writer and his donkey. Like so many, he was forced into exile by the Spanish Civil War.

Rafael Alberti (1902-99), member of the so-called 'Generation of '27', another loose grouping of artists and writers, was a poet from El Puerto de Santa María and close friend of Federico García Lorca's. Achieving recognition with his first book of poems, *Mar y tierra* (later renamed *Marinero en tierra*) Alberti was a Communist (who once met Stalin) and fought on the Republican side in the Civil War. He was forced into exile at the end of the war, only returning to Spain in 1978.

Birds

Finlayson, **Clive**, *A Birdwatchers' Guide to Southern* Spain and Gibraltar, Collins.

García, **Ernest and Patterson**, **Andrew**, *Where to Watch Birds in Southern Spain*, Helm.

Palmer, **Michael**, *A Bird Watching Guide to Southern Spain*, Arlequin.

Food and drink

Casas, **Penelope**, *The Foods and Wines of Spain* (1982), Knopf. Considered by many as the definitive book on Spanish cooking, covers regional cuisine as well as tapas.

Davidson, **A**, *Guide to the Seafood of Spain and Portugal* (1992), Santana Books. A comprehensive guide to any of the finny tribes that may turn up on your plate in restaurants and tapas bars.

Read, **J**, *Wines of Spain* (2001), Mitchell Beazley. Updated edition of this good in-depth guide to Spain's wines and wineries.

Woodall, **J**, *In Search of the Firedance* (1992), Sinclair Stevenson. An excellent and impassioned history and travelogue of flamenco, if inclined to over-romanticize.

History and travel

Carr, **R** (ed), *Spain: A History* (2000), OUP. An interesting compilation of recent writing on Spanish history, with entertaining and myth-dispelling contributions from leading academics.

Elliott, **J**, *Imperial Spain* (1963), Edward Arnold. History as it should be, precise, sympathetic, and very readable.

Fletcher, **R**, *Moorish Spain* (1992), Phoenix Press. A simple and approachable history of the Moorish presence in Spain with an attempt to gauge how life was for the average citizen.

Ford, **R**, *Gatherings from Spain* (1846), John Murray Press. Superb and sweeping overview of Spanish culture and customs; surpassed by few if any travel writers since. Recently reprinted by Pallas Athene.

Jacobs, **M**, *Andalucía* (1998), Pallas Athene. An excellent series of essays and information by a British writer who knows the region deeply. Never straying into sentimentality, the author captures much of the magic and history of the region.

Thomas, **H**, *The Spanish Civil War* (1961/77), Penguin. The first unbiased account of the war read by many Spaniards in the censored Franco years, this is large but always readable. A superbly researched work.

Webster, **J**, *Duende* (2003), Doubleday. A frenetic journey through the underground world of flamenco which almost ends up consuming the author. *Andalus* (2004), Doubleday. A picaresque voyage in search of the elusive spirit of Spain.

Literature

Alberti, **R**, *Concerning the Angels* (1995), City Lights Books. Some of this writer's finest poems, written in the late 1920s.

Cohen, **J** (ed), *The Penguin Book of Spanish Verse* (1988), Penguin. Excellent collection of Spanish poetry through the ages, with original versions and transcriptions.

Jiménez, **J**, *Platero and I* (1994), Clarion. Beautifully illustrated version of this lyric prose poem about a conversation between the poet and his donkey in the streets of Moguer.

Lee, **L**, *As I Walked Out One Midsummer Morning* (1969), Penguin. A poignant account of a romantic walk across pre-Civil War Spain; traversing the country when he reached Cádiz. *A Rose in Winter* is the same author's story about returning after the war.

Language

Learning Spanish is a useful part of the preparation for a trip to Spain and no volumes of dictionaries, phrase books or word lists will provide the same enjoyment as being able to communicate directly with the people of the country you are visiting. It is definitely a good idea to make an effort to grasp the basics before you go. As you travel you will pick up more of the language and the more you know, th4 more you will benefit from your stay.

General pronunciation

For travelling purposes, everyone in Andalucía speaks Spanish, known either as *castellano* or *español*, and it's a huge help to know some. The local accent, *andaluz*, is characterized by dropping consonants left, right and centre, thus *dos tapas* tends to be *dotapa*. Unlike the rest of Spain, the letters 'C' and 'Z' in words such as aren't pronounced /th/ (although in Cádiz province, perversely, they tend to pronounce the letter 'S' with that sound.

Vowels
a as in English *cat*; **e** as in English *best*; **i** as the *ee* in Enklish *feet*; **o** as in English *shop*; **u** as the *oo* in English *food*; **ai** as the *i* in English *ride*; **ei** as *ey* in English *they*; **oi** as *oy* in English *toy*.

Consonants
Most consonants can be pronounced more or less as rhey are in English. The exceptions are:
g before *e* or *i* is the same as *j* (see below); **h** is always silent (except in *ch* as in *chair*); **j** as the *ch* in Scottish *loch*; **ll** as the *y* in *yellow*; **ñ** as the *ni* in *onion*; **rr** trilled much more than in English; **x** depending on its location, pronopunced *x*, *s*, *sh* or *j*.

Spanish words and phrases

Greetings, courtesies

hello *hola*

good morning *buenos días*

good afternoon/evening/night
buenas tardes/noches

goodbye *adiós/chao*

pleased to meet you *mucho gusto*

see you later *hasta luego*

how are you? *¿cómo está?¿cómo estás?*

I'm fine, thanks *estoy muy bien, gracias*

I'm called... *me llamo...*

what is your name? *¿cómo se llama? ¿cómo te llamas?*

yes/no *sí/no*

please *por favor*

thank you (very much) *(muchas) gracias*

I speak Spanish *hablo español*

I don't speak Spanish *no hablo español*

do you speak English? *¿habla inglés?*

I don't understand *no entiendo/no comprendo*

please speak slowly *hable despacio por favor*

I am very sorry *lo siento mucho/disculpe*

what do you want? *¿qué quiere? ¿qué quieres?*

I want *quiero*

I don't want it *no lo quiero*

leave me alone *déjeme en paz/no me moleste*

good/bad *bueno/malo*

Basic questions, words and phrases

have you got a room for two people *¿tiene una habitación para
dos personas?*

how do I get to_? *¿cómo llego a_?*

how much does it cost? *¿cuánto cuesta? ¿cuánto es?*

I'd like to make a long-distance phone call *quisiera hacer una llamada de larga distancia*

is service included? *¿está incluido el servicio?*

is tax included? *¿están incluidos los impuestos?*

when does the bus leave (arrive) *¿a qué hora sale (llega) el autobús?*

when? *¿cuándo?*

where is_? *¿dónde está_?*

where can I buy tickets? *¿dónde puedo comprar boletos?*

where is the nearest petrol station? *¿dónde está la gasolinera más cercana?*

why? *¿por qué?*

bank *el banco*

bathroom/toilet *el baño*

to be *ser, estar*

bill *la factura/la cuenta*

cash *el efectivo*

cheap *barato/a*

credit card *la tarjeta de crédito*

exchange house *la casa de cambio*

exchange rate *el tipo de cambio*

expensive *caro/a*

to go *ir*

to have *tener, haber*

market *el mercado*

note/coin *el billete/la moneda*

police (policeman) *la policía (el policía)*

post office *el correo*

public telephone *el teléfono público*

shop *la tienda*

supermarket *el supermercado*

there is/are *hay*

there isn't/aren't *no hay*

ticket office *la taquilla*
traveller's cheques *los cheques de viajero/los travelers*

Getting around
aeroplane *el avión*
airport *el aeropuerto*
arrival/departure *la llegada/salida*
avenue *la avenida*
block *la cuadra*
border *la frontera*
bus station *la terminal de autobuses/camiones*
bus *el bus/el autobús/el camión*
collective/fixed-route taxi *el colectivo*
corner *la esquina*
customs *la aduana*
first/second class *la primera/segunda clase*
left/right *izquierda/derecha*
ticket *el boleto*
empty/full *vacío/lleno*
highway, main road *la carretera*
immigration *la inmigración*
insurance *el seguro*
insured person *el asegurado/la asegurada*
to insure yourself against *asegurarse contra*
luggage *el equipaje*
motorway, freeway *el autopista/la carretera*
north, south, west, east *el norte, el sur, el oeste (occidente),
el este (oriente)*
oil *el aceite*
to park *estacionarse*
passport *el pasaporte*
petrol/gasoline *la gasolina*
puncture *el pinchazo*
street *la calle*

that way *por allí/por allá*
this way *por aquí/por acá*
tourist card/visa *la tarjeta de turista/visa*
tyre *la llanta*
unleaded *sin plomo*
waiting room *la sala de espera*
to walk *caminar/andar*

Accommodation

air conditioning *el aire acondicionado*
all-inclusive *todo incluido*
bathroom, private *el baño privado*
bed, double/single *la cama matrimonial/sencilla*
blankets *las cobijas/mantas*
to clean *limpiar*
dining room *el comedor*
guesthouse *la casa de huéspedes*
hotel *el hotel*
noisy *ruidoso*
pillows *las almohadas*
power cut *el apagón/corte*
restaurant *el restaurante*
room/bedroom *el cuarto/la habitación*
sheets *las sábanas*
shower *la ducha/regadera*
soap *el jabón*
toilet *el sanitario/excusado*
toilet paper *el papel higiénico*
towels, clean/dirty *las toallas limpias/sucias*
water, hot/cold *el agua caliente/fría*

Health

aspirin *la aspirina*
blood *la sangre*
chemist *la farmacia*
condoms *los preservativos, los condones*
contact lenses *los lentes de contacto*
contraceptives *los anticonceptivos*
contraceptive pill *la píldora anticonceptiva*
diarrhoea *la diarrea*
doctor *el médico*
fever/sweat *la fiebre/el sudor*
pain *el dolor*
head *la cabeza*
period/sanitary towels *la regla/las toallas femininas*
stomach *el estómago*

Family

family *la familia*
brother/sister *el hermano/la hermana*
daughter/son *la hija/el hijo*
father/mother *el padre/la madre*
husband/wife *el esposo (marido)/la esposa*
boyfriend/girlfriend *el novio/la novia*
friend *el amigo/la amiga*
married *casado/a*
single/unmarried *soltero/a*

Months, days and time

January *enero*
February *febrero*
March *marzo*
April *abril*

May *mayo*
June *junio*
July *julio*
August *agosto*
September *septiembre*
October *octubre*
November *noviembre*
December *diciembre*
Monday *lunes*
Tuesday *martes*
Wednesday *miércoles*
Thursday *jueves*
Friday *viernes*
Saturday *sábado*
Sunday *domingo*
at one o'clock *a la una*
at half past two *a las dos y media*
at a quarter to three *a cuarto para las tres/a las tres menos quince*
it's one o'clock *es la una*
it's seven o'clock *son las siete*
it's six twenty *son las seis y veinte*
it's five to nine *son las nueve menos cinco*
in ten minutes *en diez minutos*
five hours *cinco horas*
does it take long? *¿tarda mucho?*

Numbers
one *uno/una*
two *dos*
three *tres*
four *cuatro*
five *cinco*
six *seis*

seven *siete*

eight *ocho*
nine *nueve*
ten *diez*
eleven *once*
twelve *doce*
thirteen *trece*
fourteen *catorce*
fifteen *quince*
sixteen *dieciséis*
seventeen *diecisiete*
eighteen *dieciocho*
nineteen *diecinueve*
twenty *veinte*
twenty-one *veintiuno*
thirty *treinta*
forty *cuarenta*
fifty *cincuenta*
sixty *sesenta*
seventy *setenta*
eighty *ochenta*
ninety *noventa*
hundred *cien/ciento*
thousand *mil*

Food glossary

Food and tapas

aceite	oil; *aceite de oliva* is olive oil
aceitunas	olives; the best kind are *manzanilla*
acelga	beet/chard
adobo	marinated fried nuggets usually of shark; delicious
aguacate	avocado

ahumado	smoked; *tabla de ahumados* is a mixed plate of smoked fish
ajo	garlic; *ajetes* are young garlic shoots
ajo arriero	a simple sauce of garlic, paprika and parsley
albóndigas	meatballs
alcachofa	artichoke
alcaparras	capers
aliño	a salad, often of egg or potato, with chopped onion, peppers and tomato with salt, vinegar and olive oil.
alioli	a tasty sauce made from raw garlic blended with oil and egg yolk
almejas	small clams
alubias	broad beans
anchoa	preserved anchovy
añejo	aged (of cheeses, rums, etc)
angulas	baby eels
anís	aniseed
arroz	rice; *arroz con leche* is a sweet rice pudding
asado	roast; an *asador* is a restaurant specializing in charcoal-roasted meat and fish
atún	blue-fin tuna
azúcar	sugar
bacalao	salted cod
berberechos	cockles
berenjena	aubergine/eggplant
besugo	red bream
bistek	steak: *poco hecho* is rare, *al punto* is medium rare, *regular* is medium, *muy hecho* is well-done
bizcocho	sponge cake or biscuit

bocadillo/bocata	a crusty filled roll
bogavante	lobster
bonito	a small, tasty tuna fish
boquerones	fresh anchovies, often served filleted in garlic and oil
botella	bottle
brasa (a la)	cooked on a griddle over coals
brochetas de pescado	fish kebab
buey	ox
cabrales	pungent goat cheese from Asturias
cabrito	kid
cacahuetes	peanuts
calamares	squid
caldereta	a stew of meat or fish usually made with sherry.
caldo	a thickish soup
callos	tripe
cangrejo	crab; occasionally river crayfish
caracol	snail
caramelos	sweets
carne	meat
carillada	cheek and jowls of the pig or cow
castañas	chestnuts
cazuela	a stew, often of fish or seafood
cebolla	onion
centollo	spider crab
cerdo	pork
ceviche	shellfish salad marinated in lime juice
champiñon	mushroom
chipirones (*en su tinta*)	small squid, often served in its own ink deliciously mixed with butter and garlic
choco	cuttlefish
chorizo	spicy red sausage

chuleta/chuletilla	chop
chuletón	T-bone steak, often sold by weight
churrasco	barbecued meat, often ribs with a spicy sauce
churro	a fried dough-stick usually eaten with hot chocolate, *chocolate con churros*
cigala	the four-wheel drive of the prawn world, with pincers
cochinillo	roast suckling pig
cocido	a heavy stew, usually of meat and chickpeas/beans
codorniz	quail
cogollo	lettuce heart
conejo	rabbit
congrio	conger-eel
cordero	lamb
corvina	meagre fish
costillas	ribs
crema catalana	a lemony crème brûlée
croquetas	deep-fried crumbed balls of meat, béchamel, seafood or vegetables
dátiles	dates
dorada	a species of bream (gilthead)
dulce	sweet
embutido	any salami-type sausage
empanada	a savoury pie, either pasty-like or in flat tins and sold by the slice.
ensalada	salad; *mixta* is usually a large portion of a bit of everything
ensaladilla rusa	Russian salad, potato, peas and carrots in mayonnaise
escabeche	pickled in wine and vinegar
espárragos	asparagus, white and usually canned
espinacas	spinach

estofado	braised, often in stew form
fabada	famous Asturian stew of beans, *chorizo* and *morcilla*
fideuá	a bit like a paella but with noodles
flambeado	flambéed
flamenquín	a fried and crumbed finger of meat stuffed with ham
flan	the ubiquitous crème caramel, great when home made (*casero*), awful out of a plastic cup.
frambuesas	raspberries
fresas	strawberries
frito/a	fried
fruta	fruit
galletas	biscuits
gambas	prawns
garbanzos	chickpeas
gazpacho	a cold, garlicky tomato soup
granizado	popular summer drink, like a frappé fruit milkshake
guisado/guiso	stewed/a stew
guisantes	peas
habas	broad beans, often deliciously stewed with ham
harina	flour
helado	icecream
hígado	liver
hojaldre	puff pastry
horno (al)	oven (baked)
hueva	fish roe
huevo	egg
huevos a la flamenca	eggs fried in a terracotta dish with a spicy mixture of tomato and ham
huevos de codorniz	quails' eggs

235

jamón	ham: *jamón de York* is cooked ham, much better is the cured *serrano*.
judías verdes	green beans
langosta	crayfish
langostinos	king prawns
lechazo	milk-fed lamb
lechuga	lettuce
lengua de almendra	a small tongue-shaped almond cake
lenguado	sole
lentejas	lentils
limón	lemon
lomo	loin, usually sliced pork
longaniza	a long sausage, speciality of Aragón
lubina	sea bass
macedonia de frutas	fruit salad, usually tinned
macerado	marinated
manchego	Spain's national cheese; hard, whiteish and made from ewe's milk
mantequilla	butter
manzana	apple
mariscos	shellfish
mechada	(minced) meat
mejillones	mussels
melocotón	peach, usually served in syrup
melva	mackerel, often served semi-dried
menestra	a vegetable stew, usually served like a minestrone without the liquid and often seeded with ham and pork
menú	a set meal, usually three or more courses, bread and wine or water
menudo	tripe stew, usually with chickpeas and mint
merluza	hake

miel	honey
migas	breadcrumbs, fried and often mixed with lard and meat
mojama	cured tuna meat
mollejas	sweetbreads; ie the pancreas of a calf or lamb
montadito	a small, toasted filled roll
morcilla	blood sausage
morro	cheek: pork or lamb
mostaza	mustard
naranja	orange
nata	sweet, whipped cream
natillas	rich custard dessert
navajas	razor-shells
nécora	small sea crab (velvet crab)
nueces	walnuts
orejas	ears, usually of a pig
ostra	oyster
pan	bread
panes	tasty open sandwiches
parrilla	grill; a *parrillada* is a mixed grill
pastel	cake/pastry
patatas	potatoes; often chips, *patatas fritas*; *bravas* are with spicy sauce
pato	duck
pavía	a crumbed and fried nugget of fish
pavo	turkey
pechuga	breast (usually chicken)
perdiz	partridge
pescado	fish
pestiños	an Arabic-style confection of pastry and honey, traditionally eaten during *Semana Santa*
pez espada	swordfish

picadillo	a dish of spicy mincemeat
picante	hot, ie spicy
pichón	squab
picos	breadsticks
pimienta	pepper
pimientos	peppers
pinchito de lomo	a small pork kebab
piña	pineapple
pipas	sunflower seeds, a common snack
plancha (a la)	grilled on a hot iron or pan fried
plátano	banana
pollo	chicken
postre	dessert
pringá	a tasty paste of stewed meats usually eaten in a *montadito* and a traditional final tapa of the evening
puerros	leeks
pulpo	octopus
puntillitas	small prawns, often served crumbed
queso	cheese
rabo de buey/toro	oxtail
ración	a portion of food served in cafés and bars; check the size and order a half (*media*) if you want less
rana	frog; *ancas de rana* is frogs' legs
rape	monkfish/anglerfish
relleno/a	stuffed
revuelto	scrambled eggs
riñones (al Jerez)	kidneys (stewed in sherry)
rodaballo	turbot, pricey and toothsome
romana (a la)	fried in batter
sal	salt
salchichón	salami
salmón	salmon

salmorejo	a thicker version of *gazpacho*
salpicón	seafood salad with onion and vinegar
San Jacobo	a steak cooked with ham and cheese
sardiñas	sardines, delicious grilled
seco	dry
secreto	a grilled or fried piece of pork loin
sepia	cuttlefish
serrano	see jamón
setas	wild mushrooms
solomillo	beef fillet steak from the sirloin bone
sopa	soup
surtido de queso/jamón	platter of cheeses or ham
tajines	a Moroccan stew typically of lamb with fruit such as plums or apples.
tarta	tart or cake
ternera	veal or young beef
toclnillo de cielo	an excellent caramelized egg dessert
tocino	pork lard
tomate	tomato
torrijas	bread fried in milk and covered in honey and cinnamon
tortilla	a Spanish omelette
tostada	toast
trucha	trout
urta	red-banded sea bream
uva	grape
venao/venado	venison
verduras	vegetables
vieiras	scallops, also called *veneras*
yema	a rich egg-based pastry
zanahoria	carrot

Drink

agua (mineral con gas/ sin gas)	water (mineral sparkling/still)
cachaça	a white cane spirit, like white rum
café	coffee: solo is black, served espresso-style, cortado adds a dash of milk, con leche more and americano is a long black coffee.
caña	draught beer
cava	sparkling wine
cerveza	beer
chocolate	a popular afternoon drink; also slang for hashish
chupitos	shooters (cocktails or straight spirits)
fino	the classic dry sherry
leche	milk
manzanilla	the dry, salty sherry from Sanlúcar de Barrameda. Also, confusingly, camomile tea and a type of olive
mosto	grape juice, a common option in bars
orujo	a fiery grape spirit, often brought to add to black coffee
rebujito	a mix of manzanilla and lemonade
sidra	cider
té	tea
vaso	glass
vino (tinto, blanco)	wine (red, white); rosado or clarete is rosé; a tinto de verano is mixed with lemonade and ice
zumo	juice, usually bottled and pricey

Architecture glossary

alcázar	a Moorish fort
apse	a vaulted square or rounded recess at the back end of a church or chapel
archivolt	decorative carving around the outer surface of an arch
artesonado ceiling	ceiling of carved wooden panels with Islamic motifs popular throughout Spain in the 15th and 16th centuries.
azulejo	an ornamental ceramic tile
baldacchino	an ornate carved canopy above an altar or tomb; typical of Galicia
bodega	a cellar where wine is kept or made; also modern winery or wine shop
capilla	a chapel within a church or cathedral
capital	the top of a column, joining it to another section, often highly decorated
castillo	a castle or fort
catedral	a cathedral, ie the seat of a bishop
Churrigueresque	a particularly ornate form of Spanish baroque, named after the Churriguera brothers
colegiata	a collegiate church, ie one ruled by a chapter of canons
convento	a monastery or convent
coro	the area enclosing the choirstalls, often central and completely closed off in Spanish churches
cuisson	points where the beams intersect in a coffered ceiling: frequently decorated with shields
ermita	a hermitage or rural chapel

hospital	in pilgrimage terms, a place where pilgrims used to be able to rest, receive nourishment and receive medical attention
iglesia	church
lobed arch	a Moorish arch with depressions in the shape of simple arches
lonja	a guildhall or fish market
mihrab	a central niche in a mosque, always aligned towards Mecca and the focus for worshippers' prayers
mocárabes	small concave spaces in Moorish ceilings
modernista	a particularly imaginative variant of art nouveau that came out of Catalunya; exemplified by Gaudí
monasterio	a large monastery usually located in a rural area
monstrance	a ceremonial container for displaying the host
mozarabic	the style of Christian artisans living under Moorish rule
mudéjar	the work of Muslims living under Christian rule after the reconquest, characterized by ornate brickwork
multifoil	a word describing a type of Muslim-influenced arch with consecutive circular depressions
muralla	city walls

Index

Credits

Footprint credits

Text editor: Felicity Laughton
Picture editor: Kevin Feeney
Map editor: Sarah Sorensen
Assistant editor: Sophie Pitt

Publisher: Patrick Dawson
Series created by: Rachel Fielding
In-house cartography: Claire Benison,
Kevin Feeney, Robert Lunn, Angus
Dawson
Design: Mytton Williams
Maps: Footprint Handbooks Ltd

Print

Manufactured in Italy by LegoPrint
Pulp from sustainable forests

Photography credits

Front cover: Powerstock
Inside: Alamy
Generic Images: John Matchett
Back cover: Alamy

Footprint feedback

We try as hard as we can to make
each Footprint guide as up to date as
possible, but, of course, things always
change. If you want to let us know
about your experiences – good, bad
or ugly – then don't delay, go to
www.footprintbooks.com and send
us your comments.

Publishing information

Footprint Costa de la Luz
1st edition
Text and maps © Footprint Handbooks
Ltd, March 2005

ISBN 1 904777 31 7
CIP DATA: a catalogue record for this
book is available from the British Library

Published by Footprint
6 Riverside Court
Lower Bristol Road
Bath, BA2 3DZ, UK
T +44 (0)1225 469141
F +44 (0)1225 469461
discover@footprintbooks.com
www.footprintbooks.com

Distributed in the USA by
Publishers Group West

Complete title list

Latin America & Caribbean

Antigua & Leeward Islands (P)
Argentina
Barbados (P)
Bolivia
Brazil
Caribbean Islands
Central America & Mexico
Chile
Colombia
Costa Rica
Cuba
Cusco & the Inca Trail
Dominican Republic (P)
Ecuador & Galápagos
Guatemala
Havana (P)
Mexico
Nicaragua
Peru
Patagonia
Rio de Janeiro (P)
St Lucia (P)
South American Handbook
Venezuela

North America

New York (P)
Vancouver (P)
Western Canada

Africa

Cape Town (P)
East Africa
Egypt
Libya
Marrakech (P)
Morocco
Namibia
South Africa
Tunisia
Uganda

Middle East

Dubai (P)
Israel
Jordan
Syria & Lebanon

Asia

Bali
Bangkok & the Beaches
Bhutan
Cambodia
Goa
Hong Kong (P)
India
Indian Himalaya
Indonesia
Laos
Malaysia
Myanmar (Burma)
Nepal
Northern Pakistan
Pakistan
Rajasthan
Singapore
South India
Sri Lanka
Sumatra
Thailand
Tibet
Vietnam

Australasia

Australia
East Coast Australia
New Zealand
Sydney (P)
West Coast Australia

Europe

Andalucía
Barcelona
Berlin (P)
Bilbao (P)
Bologna (P)
Cardiff and South Wales (P)
Copenhagen (P)
Costa de la Luz (P)
Croatia
Dublin (P)
Edinburgh (P)
England
Glasgow (P)
Ireland
London
London (P)
Madrid (P)
Naples (P)
Northern Spain
Paris (P)
Reykjavik (P)
Scotland
Scotland Highlands & Islands
Seville (P)
Spain
Tallinn (P)
Turin (P)
Turkey
Valencia (P)
Verona (P)

(P) - pocket Handbook

Lifestyle guides

Surfing Europe

Publishing stuff

247

For a different view…
choose a Footprint

Over 100 Footprint travel guides
Covering more than 150 of the world's most exciting
countries and cities in Latin America, the Caribbean, Africa, Indian
sub-continent, Australasia, North America, Southeast Asia, the
Middle East and Europe.

Discover so much more…
The finest writers. In-depth knowledge. Entertaining and accessible.
Critical restaurant and hotels reviews. Lively descriptions of all the
attractions. Get away from the crowds.

Map 1 Cádiz

Bahía de Cádiz

Plaza Argüelles

Alameda Marqués de Comillas

Alameda Apodaca

Museo de Cádiz

Plaza San Francisco

Plaza de la Mina

Carmen

Calderón de la Barca

General Menacho

Santiago Terry

Ahumada

Zorilla

Buenos Aires

Antonio López

Adolfo de Castro

Vea Murguía

Fermín Caballero

Isabel

Bendición de Dios

San Isidro

Paseo Carlos III

Manuel Rancés

Botica

Sagasta

Sacramento

San Pedro

Presidente Rivadavia

Cánovas del Castillo

Plaza Mentidero

Veedor

Cervantes

Plata

Ancha

Junquera

Plaza San Antonio

San Antonio

Torre

Zaragoza

Centro de Salud

Multicines El Centro

Parque Genovés

Bartolomé Llompart

Hercules

las Navas

Ceballos

Viudas

San Dimas

San Telmo

Soledad

Benjumeda

M de Real Tesoro

Plaza Falla

Santa Inés

Torre de Tavira

Paseo Santa Bárbara

Av Dr Gómez Ulla

Santa Rosalía

Gran Teatro Falla

Oratorio San Felipe Neri

Museo de las Cortes

Plaza de las Flores/Plaza Topete

B Pérez Galdós

Sacramento

Sotano

Obispo Calvo y Valero

Santa Lucía

Robles

Plaza Libertad

Libertad

Campo de las Balas

Felipe Abarzuza

Doctor Marañón

Guatemala

Bolivia

San Rafael

Diego Arias

Jesús Nazareno

Encarnación

Armengual

Mateo de Alba

Sagasta

Cruz

San Vicente

Pasquín

Mattas

Barquillas de Lope

Rosa

Martínez Campos

Belén

Pastora

Paz

María Arteaga

José

Castillo de Santa Catalina

Av Duque Nájera

José Celestino Mutis

Patrocinio

Trinidad

Jovellar

Virgen de la Palma

Corralón de los Carros

BARRIO DE LA VIÑA

Puerto Chico

Playa de la Caleta

Poller

Paraguay

Angel

Perición de Cádiz

Venezuela

San Félix

Virgen de la Palma

Profesor Atcma Quesada

Arrufuz

Doctores Meléndez

Castillo de San Sebastián

250

Puerto de la Caleta

Campo del Sur

Av. del Duque de Nájera

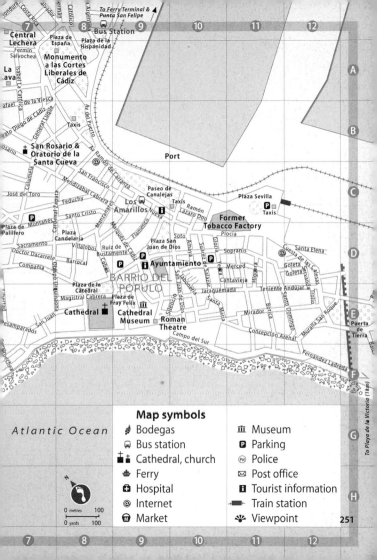

Atlantic Ocean

Map symbols

🍷	Bodegas		🏛	Museum
🚍	Bus station		🅿	Parking
✝✝	Cathedral, church		🅟	Police
⛴	Ferry		✉	Post office
✚	Hospital		ℹ	Tourist information
@	Internet		🚈	Train station
🏪	Market		�֍	Viewpoint

To Ferry Terminal &
Punta San Felipe

Bus Station

Central
Lechera

Fermín
Salvochea

Plaza de
España

Plaza de la
Hispanidad

La
Cava

Isabel la Católica

Monumento
a las Cortes
Liberales de
Cádiz

Rafael de la Viesca

Beato Diego de Cádiz

General Luque

Av. del Puerto

Taxis

San Rosario &
Oratorio de la
Santa Cueva

Columela

Cardenal Zapata

Rosario

Av. Ramón de Carranza

Port

San Francisco

Mendizábal Cabrera

Feduchy

José del Toro

Plaza de
Montañés

Santo Cristo

Manuel Rancés

Marqués de Cádiz

Flamenco

Paseo de
Canalejas

Los
Amarillos

Taxis

Ramón
Lázaro Dou

Plaza Sevilla

Taxis

Former
Tobacco Factory

Plocia

Plaza de
Palillero

Sacramento

Doctor Dacarrete

Compañía

Cardenal Zapata

Barrocal

Villalobos

Plaza
Candelaria

Ruiz de
Bustamante

Soto

Plaza San
Juan de Dios

Ayuntamiento

Amaya

Suárez de Salazar

Sopranis

Cuesta de las Calesas

Santa Elena

Merced

Goleta

Goleta

Cervantes

Tolta

BARRIO DEL
POPULO

San Juan de Dios

Sagasta

Silencio

Cantaveja

Jaraquemada

Higuera

Santo Domingo

Botica

Teniente Andújar

Plaza de la
Catedral

Magistral Cabrera

Cathedral

Plaza de
Fray Félix

Cathedral
Museum

Roman
Theatre

Santa María

Campo del Sur

Mirador

Concepción Arenal

Muralla San Roque

Puerta
de
Tierra

San Juan

Desamparados

Fernández Ladreda

To Playa de la Victoria (1km)

N

0 metres 100

0 yards 100

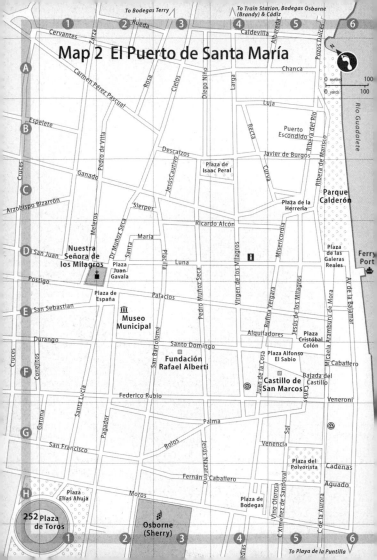

Map 2 El Puerto de Santa María

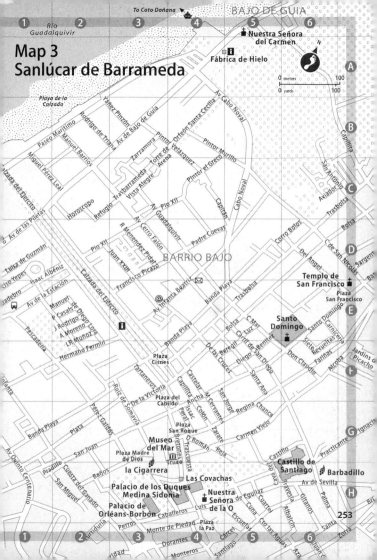

Map 3
Sanlúcar de Barrameda

To Coto Doñana

Río Guadalquivir

Nuestra Señora del Carmen

Fábrica de Hielo

0 metres 100
0 yards 100

Playa de la Calzada

BARRIO BAJO

Templo de San Francisco

Plaza San Francisco

Santo Domingo

Plaza Cisnes

Plaza del Cabildo

Plaza San Roque

Museo del Mar

Plaza Madre de Dios

la Cigarrera

Las Covachas

Palacio de los Duques Medina Sidonia

Palacio de Orléans-Borbón

Nuestra Señora de la O

Castillo de Santiago

Barbadillo

Av de Sevilla

Plaza la Paz

253

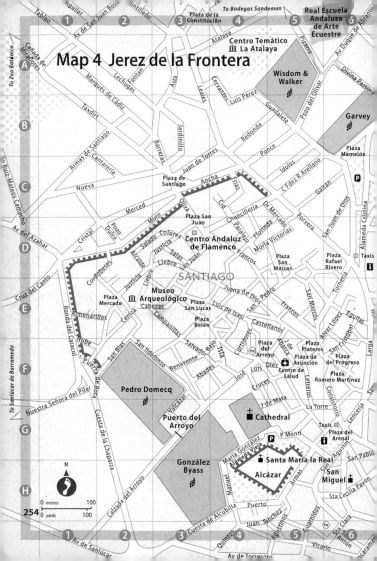

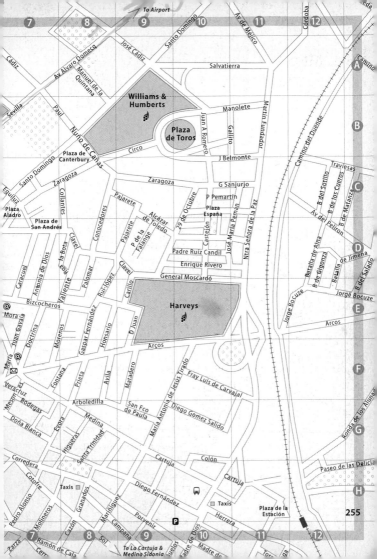

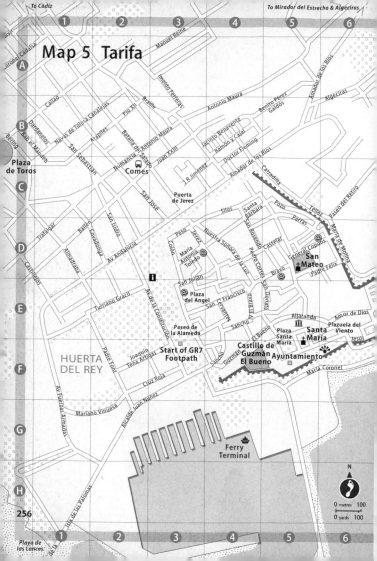

Map 5 Tarifa

Coronel Cadalso

Manuel Reine

Callao

Infanta Ferreras

Braille

Antonio Maura

Amador de los Ríos

Algeciras

Benito Pérez Galdós

Jacinto Benavente

Ramón y Cajal

Dardanelos

Bailén del Mando

Navas de Tolosa Canalejas

Pío XII

Batalla de Antonio Maura

Juan XXIII

R. Jiménez

Doctor Fleming

Amador de los Ríos

San Sebastián

Arapiles

Numancia

Comes

Plaza de Toros

San José

Puerta de Jerez

Citadilla

Silos

Santa Bárbara

Pozo

Parras

Tellez

Paseo del Retiro

San Isidro

Covadonga

Peso

Jerez

Nuestra Señora de la Luz

San Rosendo

Castelar

General Copons

San Mateo

María de Molina

Trafalgar

Bailén

Av Andalucía

Colón

María Antonia Toledo

Pedro Cortés

Bravo

Padre Félix

Almadraba

Castillejos

Turriano Gracil

Av de la Constitución

San Julián

Plaza del Angel

San C. Francisco

San Cervantes

San Donato

El Bueno

Aljaranda

Amor de Dios

Paseo de la Alameda

Sancho

Plaza Santa María

Santa María

Plazuela del Viento

Jesús

HUERTA DEL REY

Padre Font

Joaquín Tena Artigas

Start of GR7 Footpath

Sancho

Guzmán

Castillo de Guzmán El Bueno

Ayuntamiento

María Coronel

Cruz Roja

Mariano Vinuesa

Alcalde Juan Núñez

Av Fuerzas Armadas

Isla de las Palomas

Ferry Terminal

N

0 metres 100
0 yards 100

256

Playa de las Lances